CONTENTS

DEDICATION

To
Harry A. Skinner
and other pioneer missionaries
who gave of their health
a willing sacrifice
wholly acceptable to God
and to
Dorothy,
Harry's friend
and mine

INDIA!

1 THESE DAYS it would be called cultural shock, but that term was unknown back in 1915 when Harry Skinner and his three companions stood on the dock and gazed at Calcutta's bustling waterfront.

If it had not been for the comforting sight of British and Eurasian officials here and there and the reassuring sounds of spoken English, Harry might have fled back up the gangplank.

Never in all his 21 years had he seen so many dark-skinned people. Never had he heard such a babble of foreign tongues. Never had he felt so apprehensive and alien.

"So this is India." He spoke boldly to cover up his feelings. "What do you think of it?"

"Bit overpowering." Lanky Charlie Stafford ran his finger between his neck and his stiffly starched shirt collar. "Didn't think it'd be as hot as this."

"Take a look at that——" Frank Butler nodded toward the gate, where a hideously deformed child whimpered for alms. "They say the parents maim them on purpose, so they earn more money begging."

A shudder ran through the group. As one man, they felt in their pockets, and Roy Thrift dropped the handful of coins he had gathered into the beggar-child's tin.

Harry looked about him. Hundreds of half-naked coolies swarmed to and from the ship's hold. Strident-voiced food-and-drink vendors roved back and forth calling their wares.

Satin-black crows squawked and fluttered, challenging slinking, mangy dogs for choice scraps of offal.

It had all sounded so exciting when the manager of the Signs Publishing Company, together with the Australasian Union Conference committee, suggested that a group of young men go to India and do colporteur work.

"We'll draw up a contract. You sell £1,600 worth of books, and we'll take up a special Sabbath school offering to pay your return fares and other expenses. The brethren in India are pleading for canvassers to come and open up our work in the large cities."

"How long do you think it will take to sell that amount of books?"

"Possibly three years."

For various reasons, only three young men accepted the offer. A fourth, Frank Butler, was appointed to take another man's place while the missionary was on furlough. All the way across the Indian Ocean four young men had bubbled over with plans.

Now they were here, and Harry wondered whether the others felt as unsure as he did.

"I hope there's someone to meet us." Roy claimed his luggage from the customs office and watched helplessly as a yelling coolie wrestled it from his grasp and then hoisted it onto his bullet-hard head.

Other coolies elbowed their way in, grabbed the rest of the luggage, and trotted off with it.

"Follow them," Charlie shouted. "Those fellows might be thieves."

In a panic, the four pushed through the milling crowd, struggling to keep the loaded coolies in sight. At the customs shed a thin, white-suited man with an American accent held out his hand.

"Are you the colporteurs from Australia?"

"Yes, we are." Relief refreshed Harry like a cooling shower.

Introductions followed and the missionary guided them to the street, where the coolies were already loading their bags and boxes into a pair of horse-drawn gharries. The

shouting and arguing accompanying that simple operation
sounded like a prelude to violence, but the missionary
appeared undisturbed.

"All aboard." He signaled two of the young men to join
him, and the other two climbed into the second gharry.
"We'll leave your luggage at the mission office, then I'll take
you to a restaurant for some food. You must be starving
after that long wait at the dock."

Harry never forgot his first Indian meal. The missionary
assured the newcomers that the food was vegetarian, because Hindus are vegetarian by religion. But he did not
forewarn them of the fiery potency of Indian spices.

Harry put a heaped forkful of curry and rice into his
mouth and instantly felt that his head was on fire. His
tongue burned, tears streamed from his eyes, he coughed
and choked in frantic indecision whether to spit the burning
food back onto his plate at the risk of bad manners or to
endure the agony and swallow it. He decided on the latter
course, gulping and choking as the hot curry burned all the
way down to his stomach.

"Chili too hot for you?" the missionary inquired sympa-
thetically.

Harry nodded. He suspected that their host was secretly
enjoying their discomfiture and that a meal such as this was
a sort of ritual initiation accorded to all newcomers.

"Chilly!" Charlie spluttered. "There's nothing chilly
about this!"

"Oh, you'll get used to eating curry," the missionary
shrugged. "You'll have to. It's the national dish, and you
can't get anything else in most places—unless you want to
subsist on plain boiled rice and chapatties."

"What's a chapatty?"

The missionary described the leathery, whole-wheat
pancakes and then went on to tell them much more about
the Indian peoples and their customs.

For hours they sat, elbows on table, sipping cold water
brought to them by magnificently uniformed bearers. The
conversation drifted from one fascinating topic to another
until finally the missionary said, "Well, we'd better go and

find you some lodgings, and a pandit to teach you Hindustani. You'll be selling books to English-speaking people, of course, but it's wise to have some understanding of the most common language. All English officials study language. It is expected of them. We can only allow you a month, so you'll have to study hard."

Harry did not find language study such a mind-boggling chore as did his companions. Nevertheless, he was just as eager as they to take a rare hour out from their sessions with the pandit and explore the city.

They hired rickshaws and visited some of the famous temples, marveling to one another at the droves of people queuing up to reverently stroke the feet of Kali, the three-eyed, four-armed goddess of destruction.

One dawn found them at the Hooghly River watching thousands of Hindus take a ritual bath and worship the rising sun. The sight of men neck deep in the river, gulping great mouthfuls of the muddy water while their neighbors soaped and rinsed themselves, and a few yards away a bloated corpse floated downstream, made Harry's stomach churn.

"How can they drink it?" he choked. "That water must be thick with germs!"

"They believe that nothing but blessing comes from the holy river," the missionary said. "No wonder there's so much cholera and typhoid."

Harry and his friends rejoiced when their short training period ended and they set out to sell *Heralds of the Morning,* a book written by A. O. Tait. They were moderately successful, and found none of the religious bigotry that is present in some countries. Besides, white men selling books were a novelty, and a lot of their contacts were too polite to refuse to buy from them.

After a few months' work, the young men became so confident that they agreed to split up. Roy went across to the west coast to canvass in Bombay; Harry headed north.

Now's my chance to see the Indian countryside. Harry grinned complacently as he settled himself in a corner of a third-class compartment of the Delhi Express. Only the lowest castes traveled third class. The crowded carriages were suffocatingly hot, the unpadded wooden seats painfully hard. But Seventh-day Adventist colporteurs were too poor to travel by any but the cheapest means.

As the train chugged on its sooty way, Harry found the countryside teeming with surprises. Shiny black buffaloes wallowed in lily-decked pools. Farmers used oxen, and sometimes cows, to draw their primitive wooden plows. Women, straight as saplings, wrapped to the eyes in dingy cotton saris, moved along the verges of fields carrying enormous headloads of firewood. Mixed herds of sheep and goats nibbled their way across fields that looked as barren as a tennis court.

When night fell Harry kept his nose pressed to the grimy glass. He spurned sleep in case he might miss something interesting. The pale sickle moon in the violet sky did nothing to help him identify weird black shapes flying past the train windows, and after a couple of hours he gave in.

Inside the crowded compartment his traveling companions pulled their threadbare cotton shawls over their heads and curled up into snoring bundles. The light was too dim for reading. Harry yawned and fidgeted, folded and unfolded his arms, tried to stretch his cramped legs. Finally, he bunched up uncomfortably in his corner and closed his eyes.

When he opened them again the guard was calling, "All out for Delhi."

THE DEVIL'S MAN

2 "HAVE YOU met Angelo yet?"

"Have you come across Angelo?"

"Did you sell any books to Angelo?"

At every house a similar question greeted Harry, until his curiosity bubbled over. Who was this Angelo? Why was he so well known to all the townsfolk? Why was everyone so eager for Harry to meet him?

Most of the inhabitants of this railway town, which was thirteen miles from Delhi, were Eurasians. Many of them ordered the book *Heralds of the Morning.* All of them asked Harry whether he had met Angelo.

"No," Harry answered his latest questioner, "but I want to meet him. He must be a very famous person for everyone to know him so well."

"Oh, he is." The man's lips curved in a strange sort of smile. "Go down to the railway sheds and you'll find him. He's an engine cleaner."

Harry raised his eyebrows, but said nothing. Engine cleaning was a very humble occupation for such a well-known person, and it made him all the more curious to meet Angelo.

Tucking his prospectus into his bag, he said goodbye to the man and set off toward the railway sheds. He might as well go and meet Angelo right now. Then, when people asked him whether he had seen Angelo, he could tell them he had.

Harry jogtrotted down the steep embankment in the

merciless midday sun. The fierce glare reflecting from the gleaming tracks hurt his eyes, and he was glad to step inside the huge, dark sheds that housed the idle engines. As his eyes adjusted to the gloom he saw a young man in greasy overalls coming toward him.

"Are you Mr. Angelo?"

"Yes." The handsome young Italian flashed a beaming smile. "I am Angelo. Everyone knows me."

"So it seems." Harry smiled and introduced himself. "I'm selling books, and in every house I've been to someone has asked me whether I've met Angelo. They got me so curious I just had to come and meet you."

"Fine, come up to my house." Angelo wiped his hands on an oily rag and threw it aside. "I've finished this engine, and it's about time for my lunch and siesta anyway. Come along, and I will tell you why everyone knows me."

He led the way along a short, rough track to the bachelors' quarters and opened the door for Harry to precede him. Harry stepped inside and then blinked in astonishment. He had expected the front room to be furnished like most of the other Anglo-Indian front rooms: A small table covered with an embroidered cloth and surmounted by "holy" pictures and stiffly posed photographs of numerous relatives, fat padded chairs, floor rugs, vases of dusty artificial flowers, gay floral curtains across the doorways, and pictures and pictures and more pictures. Instead, the floor space around the perimeter of the room was taken up by an assortment of clay pots, some small enough to hold about a gallon of liquid, others large enough to hold thirty or forty gallons. Shelves around the walls held wicker baskets of all shapes and sizes. A plain deal table and two wooden chairs in the middle of the room comprised the sole furniture.

Angelo caught Harry's astonished stare and his black eyes twinkled. "You like my furnishings, yes?"

"They are rather—different," Harry said tactfully. "What's in all those pots and baskets?"

"Snakes."

"Snakes!"

"Yes. Now you sit on this chair, and I'll show you some-

Harry stared in horrified fascination as Angelo casually handled the deadly snakes.

thing that not many others have seen. Keep still and don't panic or you'll be a dead man. Most of these are poisonous snakes, and their fangs and poison sacs are still intact." Angelo reached into one of the clay jars and pulled out a yellow-and-black banded krait. "See, if this one bit you, you'd be finished inside of ten minutes."

Harry stared in horrified fascination as the serpent twined itself around Angelo's arm and hand and then slid sinuously onto the cement floor. He did not need to be told twice. Keeping his legs tucked under him on the chair he watched in frozen fear while Angelo went around the room upturning pots and unfastening baskets until the whole floor was alive with a crawling mass of hissing, writhing, wriggling snakes. Angelo stepped fearlessly among them, picking up a hooded cobra for Harry to admire, flicking down a slender green tree snake when it curled inquisitively around the table leg, draping a huge python around his shoulders and staggering around the room bent under its weight.

"I can do anything with these snakes," he boasted, taking a snake-charmer's gourd pipe from a shelf. "Watch."

Squatting down, he began blowing through the strange instrument, and at the sound some of the snakes reared up and swayed to and fro in time to the rhythm, their beady eyes fastened hypnotically on his moving hands.

The fetid air inside the closed room was oven hot, yet Harry shivered and goose pimples prickled his skin. He dared not speak or move lest he attract the attention of the venomous reptiles, and he breathed a sigh of pure relief when at last Angelo began gathering up his repulsive pets and sliding them back into their pots and baskets.

When the last wriggling tail disappeared, Harry examined the floor closely before unfolding his legs and standing up.

Angelo laughed at Harry's caution and ran his slender fingers through his own curly black hair. "I like you, Harry. Sit down again and I will tell you my story. Everybody knows me because I am a spiritist. I worship the devil. Not any of his evil spirits, but the devil himself. He visits me nearly every day and he tells me what to do and what not to do. Everyone in this town, European or native, is under my power. They all know me and are terrified of me.

"My house here is beside the road to the burning ghat. You know how the Hindus carry their dead on a bamboo litter, wrapped only in a sheet, and then burn them on a funeral pyre. Yes?"

Harry nodded. Many times he had stood aside to watch such processions pass, mourners carrying the corpse shoulder high, its lifeless head bobbing as they jogged along.

"You know how they always have a brass band or a lot of bagpipes accompanying the procession to scare away the evil spirits? Yes, well, whenever I hear that, I go out onto the road and the procession stops and all the people fall prostrate to the ground. They all know me."

Harry thought that Angelo sounded very proud of the

power he wielded over the townsfolk, but he did not interrupt the story.

"I have a sharp knife in my hand and I draw the cloth back from one thigh of the corpse and I cut off a piece of the dead flesh and I eat it raw, right there in front of them."

"How ghastly!" Harry recoiled in horror. "Do you like doing that?"

Angelo shuddered. "No, I loathe it. It is terrible. I dread it. But *he* tells me to do it, and I must. If I disobeyed, *he* would kill me."

Harry hardly knew what to say. Never in his life had he come in contact with such flagrant devilry, and it scared him; yet he could not leave this friendly, handsome young man without making some effort to tell him of a wonderful Saviour who could free him from the bonds of the devil. He pulled out his prospectus and launched into his canvass, praying silently that God would use his words to bring hope to this captive soul.

Angelo listened respectfully until Harry finished, but his eyes did not smile along with his lips as he said, "I'll order the book, Harry, and look through it. Maybe I can give it away to someone. I'm sure that *he* will not let me read it."

With a prayer in his heart, Harry wrote out the order and gave Angelo a receipt for his deposit. "I'll be back in six weeks to deliver your book, Angelo. Goodbye until then, and don't forget what I've told you."

India's burning sun took more than its usual toll of human life during that summer of 1916. The monsoon rains failed, and with no clouds to temper the scorching rays and no showers to cool the parching heat, man and beast alike suffered.

Constant perspiration left Harry's skin red raw with the misery of prickly heat, and the stiffly starched white suits that fashion dictated that Europeans wear added to his wretchedness, but he kept right on with his work. He not only depended on book sales for his livelihood but he felt that every book he sold spread the message of God's love in a land where a knowledge of that love was desperately needed.

Six weeks dragged by, and one morning Harry filled a large suitcase with *Heralds of the Morning,* tucked a silk handkerchief around his neck where his collar rubbed like sandpaper, protected his head with a pith helmet, and set off to deliver books in the railway township.

He was midway through his morning's work before it dawned on him that no one had mentioned Angelo, so at the next house he asked about him.

"Angelo?" The Eurasian woman looked startled. "Angelo is dead."

"Dead?" Harry echoed. "He was all right when I was here six weeks ago. I never saw a healthier young man, nor one so handsome. What did he die of?"

The woman lowered her voice and looked around as if she feared someone might hear her reply. "He didn't die of anything. The devils killed him."

Harry's face was one big question mark, and the woman beckoned him to come inside while she told what she knew. Once her tongue was loosened, she painted a lurid word picture.

"Early one morning Angelo's manservant went to his quarters to make his *pahlung ka char* [bedside tea]. He had a manservant, of course; no woman would work for him because of the snakes. Well, he opened the door, and what a sight met his eyes. The floor was covered with blood and guts. There were bits of Angelo's flesh and intestines spattered all over the room. The devils had torn him to shreds. No thief or murderer, not even a whole band of dacoits, could tear a man into little pieces like that. It was the devil."

"But why? What had Angelo done?"

"Who knows?" The woman shrugged. "He associated with the devil for a long time. Perhaps he learned too much. Or perhaps he disobeyed. Or maybe the devil tired of him. No one knows."

Scarcely believing her story, Harry thanked the woman and left. It did not seem possible that such a thing could happen. Once outside her gate he shaded his eyes and looked across the tracks to the huge railway sheds where he first met Angelo, then to the bachelors' quarters, where Angelo lived. Everything looked exactly the same as it had six weeks before. Heat waves shimmered above corrugated iron roofs; thirsty trees drooped and wilted in parched gardens; crows, gray with dust, pecked listlessly at garbage piles; and mangy pariah dogs skulked in the sparse shade of rickety fences.

No, it could not be true. After he delivered his book at the next house Harry asked the same question, "How's Angelo?"

"Angelo is no more." The man shook his head, and a doleful expression settled on his sallow face. "The devils killed him—tore him into little shreds."

"But why?"

Needing no prompting, he told the story of Angelo's demise, agreeing almost word for word with what the woman said.

Calling at house after house, Harry asked about Angelo. The Indians and Eurasians gave the same reply: "Angelo is dead. The devils killed him." Pressed for details, every account was essentially the same. It must be true.

All day Harry worked mechanically, delivering books until only one remained in his suitcase—the one that Angelo had ordered. Poor Angelo. It was no use continuing to pray for him now. Angelo was dead, and no one knew why.

Oh, yes, the townsfolk conjectured about him, made guesses, but no one would ever know exactly what happened or why. Had the devil tired of him? Or was it possible that the handsome young Italian had taken notice of Harry's words and had tried to break away from his evil master?

Harry hoped that it was so.

BURMA CALL

3 SAHARANPUR, DELHI, Lucknow, Cawnpore, Allahabad—cities made famous by the British occupation in India—Harry faithfully canvassed his way through them all. By 1917 he had easily fulfilled his contract with the Australasian Union Conference. Now he was free to return to Australia if he wished.

But the officers at the Seventh-day Adventist headquarters in India had not been blind to the success of the energetic young Australian, and one day a departmental head said to Harry, "We need someone to be field missionary secretary in Burma. Would you be interested in going there?"

Go to Burma? Harry knew that it was only fifteen years since the first Seventh-day Adventists, Meyers and Watson, had gone there to sell books among the English-speaking populace. The work in Burma was still in its infancy and it would be a real challenge. Harry liked challenges. Besides, he had no reason for rushing back to Australia right now. Why not?

"English is not as widely spoken there as it is in India. You'd need to learn Burmese."

"I think I can do that."

The transfer did not take long to arrange. Harry said goodbye to his friends in India and sailed off to Rangoon and language study.

And that was when everyone got a big surprise—including Harry himself. Young Harry Skinner proved to have a flair for languages. He learned the difficult, flowery, Burmese language with its eleven vowels and thirty-two consonants as fast as a hungry man consumes bread.

Not only did he learn to speak Burmese fluently but he could read and write the fascinating, curly script almost as easily as he could English. He outshone the other missionaries at the government examinations, and went on to take the high-proficiency tests before the Burmese Government Examining Board—and did remarkably well.

Such talent could not be wasted, and Harry soon found that he was asked to spend as much time translating as he spent training canvassers to sell books. But Harry was loath to spend his days cooped up in an office. He wanted to be out telling the Burmese people the glorious gospel story.

For the next seven years, in addition to caring for his translating commitments, Harry carried on active missionary work in many towns and country districts. Everywhere he went his fluency in Burmese, and other dialects, which he readily picked up, opened doors to him. He especially valued his contacts with the Buddhist priests, the *pongyis** who were the intelligentsia of the native population.

"Tell me about your religion," Harry invited a priest one afternoon as he sat cross-legged on the floor of an ancient monastery where a thousand gilt images of Buddha smiled inscrutably down.

The *pongyi's* keen eyes glittered. He ran a hand over his shaven head and began in a toneless voice, almost a chant, "From birth to death, life is an endless struggle toward nirvana. To gain karma one must . . ."

Harry listened patiently. His turn would come. There was nothing the monks liked better than to compare the doctrines of Christianity and Buddhism. Once he gained their confidence they talked to him for hours.

"And this good man, the only one in a wicked generation, built a large ship and saved himself and seven others from a huge flood that destroyed . . ."

---

* *pongyi* = "great glory"

Startled, Harry shook his head to clear his thoughts. The monk's droning voice and the curling wisps of incense diffusing through an atmosphere already heavy with the smell of age, made him drowse. What was it that the man said?

"And he rescued all those thousands of unhappy slaves and took them to a pleasant land where they must observe every seventh day as a holy day, and——"

"Wait a minute," Harry broke into the monk's long string of tales. "Is that story in your holy book?" He pointed to the ornate, heavy-lidded volumes of Pali scriptures piled behind the row of tiny, flickering butterlamps.

The monk caressed his hairless scalp and hitched his yellow robe over his bare shoulder. "No, these stories have been handed down from father to son for a thousand generations, perhaps a thousand thousand."

"We have those stories in our Holy Book, the Bible." Harry took out his Bible and read aloud. "You see, our forefathers—yours and mine—worshiped the same God. We are all brothers. We come from a common ancestor——"

For hours he talked, and the *pongyis** listened, their faces as expressionless as painted idols.

Harry visited other monasteries and pagodas, hundreds of them. The more he learned about their ways the more the *pongyis* trusted him. They told him secrets that no other white man knew. He heard and saw manifestations of the devil that made his spine tingle and his scalp prickle with fear.

He talked to chief abbots and monks, to squatting rows of saffron-robed novices mumbling their devotions. He pointed to the faded wall tapestries, stiff with grime, that depicted man's tortuous progress around the Wheel of Life.

"There is no need for all these vain strivings," he told them. "You can be released from evil. Jesus Christ will give you peace and hope and power. He loves you."

They gazed impassively at him. It was too easy. They had grown accustomed to their prayer wheels and penances, and few of them were willing to change.

AN ELEPHANT IN CHAINS

4 HARRY SAT hunched over the paper-littered table. Sweat dripping from the end of his nose smeared part of his writing into indecipherable blotches.

"It's no use," he sighed, running his fingers through his thick brown hair until it stood up like stubble in a hayfield. "I'll have to do a lot of thinking before I can get this passage to come right."

Today seemed to be hotter than yesterday, and yesterday hotter than the day before. Yes, and every word seemed harder to translate into Burmese than the one before it. Harry almost wished that the mission had not discovered his flair for languages, then he would not have had the task of translating scripture portions into the difficult Poh Kuhnluhn dialect.

But he didn't quite wish it, because he had long ago decided that he would do God's work whatever or wherever it may be.

"All the same," he muttered out loud, "I'd rather be on active service than poring over books and papers all day long. I'll go mad or my head will burst or something if I don't get outside for a break."

Except for the flies buzzing irritatingly around the clay pots in the kitchen, there was no one to hear or answer. Harry slammed his topee on his head, took his gun from the wall rack, and strode out into the boiling afternoon sun. He knew better than to venture outside without either hat or gun. He was not a sportsman hunter, though the jungle around teemed with wildlife. Most of the animals were harmless and more scared of him than he was of them. But he never knew when he might encounter a poisonous snake or a man-eating animal and he might have to shoot to save his life.

As the cooler shadowy jungle closed in about him, Harry relaxed into a sensitive awareness of his surroundings. Bright-red berries on a delicate creeper provided food for birds and monkeys. Shredded bark curling from a giant tree showed him where a jungle cat had sharpened its claws. He sniffed the wet, earthy smell of rotting leaf-mold underfoot, and when he halted for a moment, heard the faint skitterings and scufflings that told of lizards and other small creatures scuttling to safety at his approach.

Treading lightly and taking care not to snare his gun in looping vines, Harry the bushman was a different person from Harry the scribe. He pressed along the jungle trail until a faint clanking sound off to the right made him pause. Head cocked, he listened intently. *Clink-clank, clink-clank.* Was it some kind of birdcall that he had not heard before?

Quietly he pushed his way toward the sound. It grew louder, and suddenly he chuckled, because he recognized the sound as the clanking of an elephant's chain. Tamed elephants must be working nearby. Harry had often watched the great beasts twist their strong trunks around tall trees and wrench them out of the ground. At a word of command from their mahouts, they rolled huge logs into position, butting them with iron-hard heads or lifting them high in the air with their leathery trunks and stacking them neatly on waiting carriers as effortlessly as Harry gathered sticks of firewood.

Harry followed the clanking sound, but not until he pushed through the last clinging, thorny bush and came to a place where the undergrowth had been flattened could he see the dark-gray bulk of a huge cow elephant tethered to a stalwart tree. An incredibly small baby swayed at her side.

At the sight of Harry a trembling mahout leaped to his feet and saluted. Harry saw that he was a Manipuri tribes-

man from India. The government usually employed Mani-
puris because of their expertise in handling elephants.

"What's the trouble here?" Harry spoke in local dialect.
It had taken him only a moment to see that something was
amiss—the pitifully skinny baby, the feverishly restless
mother elephant, clanking her tethering chain, and the
mahout's obvious fear.

"Oh, Sahib, I am about to be killed!" The mahout rolled
wild, black eyes. "This elephant and its baby are about to
die, and the government officer will surely kill me."

"H'mmm." Harry knew that trained work elephants
were extremely valuable, and no doubt the government
officer would be angry, but he doubted the mahout's ex-
travagant claim. "What's gone wrong?"

"Three days ago the elephant gave birth to this baby—
such a small creature, so tiny it cannot reach up to suck its
mother's milk and so it is starving, dying. And because the
baby cannot suck her, the mother has milk fever. She is hot
and restless and getting worse by the hour. They will both
die for sure, and the government officer will kill me."

"Three days ago," echoed Harry. "Surely you could have
thought of something in that time. Why didn't you go to the
village and bring milk for the baby? I know they have cows
there and plenty of milk."

"Oh, Sahib, I couldn't do that. If I left these animals
alone for a minute, a leopard might pounce on the baby and
eat it. You know how many leopards there are in this
jungle."

Harry nodded, tapping his rifle reflectively. Yes, he knew
about the leopards. There was hardly a dog left in any
village for miles around. Daily, at dusk, the leopards crept
into the villages, seeking their favorite food, and only the
stoutest animal pen withstood their determined claws.

"Now, look here, I've thought of a plan to save you and
the elephants. You can run, can't you?"

"Like a deer, Sahib."

"All right. You run to the village and fetch a bucket of
milk, and run all the way back with it. I know you'll spill
some, but never mind, get back as fast as you can. Bring a

bottle with you, a big beer bottle would be best. I'll stay here and guard the elephants while you go. Now, run!"

The mahout dashed off down the jungle path and Harry sat on a stump with his rifle across his knees. The mother elephant stamped her feet restlessly and flapped her huge ears, twisting her head this way and that in a vain effort to see her baby. The tiny creature looked too weak to stand, and at any moment Harry expected it to topple over and die. He began to hum a hymn tune, not so loudly that he would frighten the mother elephant, but loud enough to let predators know that he was on guard.

In an incredibly short time the mahout panted back, with the bucket still two thirds full of milk and a long-necked beer bottle tucked into his loincloth.

"Right. Now have you got a funnel of some sort?"

The mahout ran to his hut and came back with a rusty tin funnel. Between them they managed to fill the bottle with milk.

"Now bring the little fellow over here in case the mother gets suspicious and tries to attack us."

The mahout put his arms around the baby elephant's middle and half-dragged, half-carried him to Harry. The little creature was too weak to protest or struggle, and they managed to push his head back and hold his trunk aside so that they could push the bottle of milk into his mouth. As soon as he tasted the milk the baby began to suck, downing bottle after bottle until the bucket was empty. The nourishment took instantaneous effect. The little animal lost his listless apathy and staggered about on wobbly legs, curling his tiny trunk around in search of more.

"That's fixed him," Harry chuckled. "Now let's see what we can do for the mother. Have you got another chain?"

"Yes, Sahib." The mahout's leathery face looked less grim. "I always keep two chains."

He disappeared into his hut and came out dragging a heavy chain. Between them they fastened the second chain to the mother elephant's front leg and secured it to another tree. Then Harry stood back and surveyed the situation. Back home in Australia he had milked hundreds of cows, but milking an elephant was a different proposition. He wondered whether anyone else had ever tried it. Cows are milked from the side, but an elephant would have to be milked between the front legs.

Conscious that the anxious eyes of the baby elephant and of the mahout centered on him, Harry cautiously approached the huge animal. One blow from her swaying trunk could kill him. But the mother elephant seemed to know that he was trying to help her and she stood still while he manipulated her swollen udder. Her teats were rock hard and Harry's efforts must have caused her pain. He prodded and punched and kneaded and finally managed to extract enough milk to soften the swollen glands a little. Triumphantly he backed away from her long tusks and grinned at the mahout.

"Now we'll build a platform so the baby can reach its mother."

Using a rusty tin funnel, they managed to fill the bottle with milk for the hungry baby elephant.

Harry skirted around the clearing, gathering armfuls of sticks and leaves, and the mahout caught the idea. He tore down branches and collected clods of dirt. Between them they pushed their materials under the elephant's chest, making a mound to raise the baby's height.

When it was completed, Harry maneuvered the baby into position and held his head back so that he could reach his mother's milk supply. As soon as he tasted the warm milk the little fellow sucked with all his might. He nuzzled his mother's belly and twitched his tiny tail in contentment. The mother stopped her restless swaying and caressed his body with her trunk.

Harry surveyed them with a satisfied smile. So did the mahout. He did not say a word of thanks, but the relief on his face was so evident that Harry grinned to himself. Well, we saved their lives, and some trouble for you, too, he thought.

As he walked back to his bungalow, Harry felt greatly refreshed, and he thanked God that he had been led to the clearing, and used to save the lives of two of God's wonderful creatures, and to help the mahout out of a bad situation.

PIG, PORCUPINE, ET CETERA, VILLAGE

5 HARRY CHUCKLED whenever he visited Wet-hpyu-ue village. Not that there was anything unusual in the village itself. It consisted of the usual huddle of bamboo huts, bony oxen, and chickens and dogs dotting the dusty paths that passed for streets. It was the name of the place that amused him. Literally translated it meant "Pig, Porcupine, et cetera."

"Why is the village called by that name?" Harry asked his friend Kothar-byaw. He was the headman, and had lived there all his life, and he ought to know. "Were there a lot of pigs and porcupines here when the place was first settled?"

Kothar-byaw shrugged. "Maybe. Pig and porcupine make good food, Thakin."

"But why the 'et cetera'"? persisted Harry. "Are all the tigers, leopards, and wild jungle animals included in the village name?"

Kothar-byaw shook his head. The village had been inhabited long before his birth, and he grew up accepting the name and never questioning its origin. Why did foreigners have to be interested in such matters?

Kothar-byaw did not realize that the more Harry learned of the Burmese language and dialects, the more he enjoyed dissecting the names of people and places, trying to find out why they had been given those names.

He already knew that many Eastern children are not given a name at birth. They are called Baby, or Little Sister,

Little Brother, Little Miss, or some other endearment. Then, when they are a few years old, their parents have a naming ceremony and the little ones are given permanent names—names that in some way reflect their developing character.

Kothar-byaw's name meant "Mr. Smooth-talk," and Harry thought that fitted him exactly. Kothar-byaw could be so smooth-tongued, so persuasive, when he wanted something. "You'd make an excellent colporteur," Harry often teased. "You could sell haircombs to bald men." But Kothar-byaw did not know what a colporteur was, so the joke fell flat.

Kothar-byaw's talk was smooth as coconut oil the day he came to Harry's bungalow and asked, "Are you very busy, Thakin? Can you listen to me a moment?"

"Yes, I am busy, but I can stop work for a while. What is it you want?"

Kothar-byaw shifted his wad of tobacco and betel nut to the other side of his mouth. He had chewed the evil stuff since he was a youngster, as evidenced by his unnaturally reddish lips and mouth and the black stains on his teeth. Harry often warned him that he would fall prey to some terrible disease if he did not stop chewing it. But his warnings fell on deaf ears, and the old Burmese continued to chew and spit out mouthfuls of saliva, crimson as blood.

"Thakin, there is an ox in the jungle; a big, wild ox that comes into our gardens and spoils them. We can only *drive* him away because we have no gun powerful enough to kill him, but with your 'spirit of death' you could easily lay him low. Then," Kothar-byaw's smooth talk dropped to a throaty whisper, "I could butcher him, skin him, cut up the meat, and sell it in the surrounding villages. I could make a fine little packet of money if you would kill that ox for me, Thakin. Will you do it?"

"Are you sure that it is a wild animal, Kothar-byaw? You're not tricking me into killing your enemy's beast?"

"Oh, no, Thakin. He's a wild one. He comes to the jungle pool not far from our village. Nearly every evening he comes to drink. You can ask the villagers."

"All right." Harry mentally reviewed his plans for the

next few weeks and decided upon a suitable day when the moon would rise before the sun set and he could see to shoot by its light if necessary. He told Kothar-byaw where to meet him, and the old chief trotted off as delighted as though the meat-sale money already jingled in his pocket.

They met on the appointed day. Kothar-byaw loaded to the headband with knife and ropes and baskets for carrying the meat; and Harry armed with his elephant gun and the clasp knife he always carried.

"This way, Thakin," Kothar-byaw choked. His flushed face and wheezing chest cold failed to cramp his enthusiasm, and he set off through the bushes, coughing as he led the way to the fringe of jungle surrounding the village. When they reached a stand of *ingyin* trees he halted. "This—is a—good—place, Thakin," he croaked, punctuating his words with harsh, racking coughs. "You—can—shoot— from here."

"All right," Harry looked around and chose a tree overlooking the route that the ox would likely take on its way to water. "You climb up into the tree and I'll wait down here."

Harry settled himself as comfortably as possible at the base of the tree, leaning against the trunk so that his back was protected from surprise attack and yet he had a clear view from both sides and front. The sun was still high and it was unlikely that any wild animals would be about, but one had to take sensible precautions.

"Shoot him—in—the chest—Thakin, so——" Kotharbyaw's cough-interspersed instructions broke off when Harry looked up and waved a threatening fist.

"Hush. The ox won't come if there's any noise."

Kothar-byaw nodded and stopped talking. But still he coughed, and the more he coughed, the more uneasy Harry became. That noise would stop any animal from coming near the water hole. He was wasting his time sitting here. He looked up into the tree again.

"It's no use staying here if you can't stop coughing, Kothar-byaw. Climb into one of the trees away over there and stuff your shirt into your mouth. Smother that cough somehow or the ox will never come today."

After Kothar-byaw's stocky form disappeared, and his incessant cough no longer fractured the silence, Harry slid the safety catch off his gun and positioned it at his side. Then, turning his head this way and that, he strained to catch the slightest sound that would indicate the ox's presence. He even sniffed the warm breeze, wishing that he had an animal's acute sense of smell. But in all that fringe of jungle he neither saw, heard, nor smelled anything to indicate the presence of any living creature other than himself.

Minute after minute ticked slowly by, and no sound disturbed the silence. The westering sun warmed and relaxed his tense body; the long period of inactivity lulled his senses; he yawned, looked at his watch, yawned again, and fell asleep.

Something—Harry never knew whether it was his sixth sense or guardian angel—jerked him back to consciousness and his startled, sleep-drugged eyes looked straight into the face of a leopard twenty paces away, staring at him with the hypnotic gaze of a cat about to spring upon a sparrow.

In shocked, split-second focus, Harry's eyes sped the length of the spotted body and centered on the twitching white tailtip, which warned him death was only seconds away. Snatching up his gun, he fired, knowing that at such close range the bullet was sure to hit the animal somewhere and praying that it might be in a fatal spot.

Without waiting to see the result of his shot he sprang to his feet and ran as if all the animals in the jungle were after him, shouting at the same time, "Kothar-byaw, help! A leopard is chasing me. Help! Help!"

As he fled, Harry fumbled to reload the "spirit of death" gun, a hard enough job in a normal situation, and now, hearing the leopard panting along behind him, and expecting any moment to feel its claws fasten into his flapping shirttail and drag him down, it seemed an impossibility. But he dare not slow down for a moment, though his thumping heart threatened to break out of his chest, and his bursting lungs seemed about to explode.

Just when he reached the limit of endurance, the bolt shot home. Harry seized the nearest bush, swung himself aside, gaining the split second needed to raise the gun in one frantic movement and fire point-blank, hitting the animal in the chest. The leopard lurched forward and fell dead at his feet. In the brief moment before it fell, Harry saw that his first shot had lamed the leopard's foreleg, otherwise it would surely have overtaken him.

Shaking with relief, he sank to his knees and thanked God for delivering him. How different the story would have been if he had not awakened, if his first panicky shot had not lamed the animal, if he had not managed to reload the gun. *If, if, if.*

"Thank You, heavenly Father. I give my worthless life back to Thee for service," he said aloud, and remained kneeling in humble consecration.

When Harry rose his first thought was for the village headman.

"Kothar-byaw," he yelled, looking across the clearing to where he had seen the headman climb into a tree. "A fine friend you are. The leopard could have killed me for all you care. Why didn't you come and help me?"

There was no answer, and Harry yelled again. Still no reply, and Harry guessed what had happened. While he slept, Kothar-byaw had become tired of waiting and crept back to his village.

He'll be angry when he hears about all the excitement he's missed, Harry grinned to himself as he unclasped his knife and prepared to skin the leopard.

He did not know much about skinning an animal so as to preserve its head and paws intact, but that did not matter because, in any case, he had no money to pay a taxidermist to mount the skin in expert fashion and fit it with gleaming glass eyes that looked ferocious as life. No, he'd have to be content to have one of the natives tan it for him so that he could have a skin rug as a memento of his adventure.

The job took longer than Harry expected, and before he heaved the bloody skin onto his shoulder he reloaded his gun and cocked it. After all the commotion the ox was not likely to venture anywhere near Wet-hpyu-ue village this evening, but he wanted to be ready just in case. One adventure a day was quite enough.

The setting sun cast long shadows over the dusty path, and as Harry neared the village, the dogs raced out, threatening the stranger with barks and bared teeth. They did not notice the leopard skin trailing over Harry's shoulder until they were quite close. When they caught the dreaded scent and tried to flee, fear paralyzed their hindquarters. The wretched, petrified creatures, yelping in terror, flailed their forelegs in the dust, vainly trying to drag their skinny bodies to safety.

Hearing all the barking and yelping, the villagers rushed out to quell the dogs with shouts and sticks, but then their mouths gaped and their hands fell to their sides. They stood stupefied watching Harry proceed down the narrow street to Kothar-byaw's house with his burden.

"See what you missed!" Harry lifted the leopard skin off his shoulder and spread it over the bamboo railing of Kothar-byaw's veranda. "If you had not sneaked off and left me you might have had the honor of killing this one."

The old chief was squatting on the veranda talking to some of his cronies, but he leapt to his feet when Harry spoke. "Where is it? Where did you leave the carcass, Thakin?" Trembling with eagerness, he reached for his knife and meat baskets.

Scarcely listening to Harry's directions, Kothar-byaw edged his way through the crowd of villagers gathering to stare at the leopard skin and ran towards the jungle. Harry knew he was after the teeth and claws of the dead animal. No charm was more efficacious in Burmese society than a leopard's tooth or claw tied around a child's neck to ward off sickness and evil. And powdered leopard's teeth were used in many of the potent cure-alls concocted by the superstitious country folk.

"Look out for the ox," Harry yelled after him. "I won't be there to save you."

But his sarcasm was lost on Mr. Smooth-talk, and after telling his story again and again, and giving the villagers enough time to admire his prize, Harry went back home for a bath and bed.

IN ELEPHANT JUNGLE

6 NO WONDER the local people refer to this as Elephant Jungle, Harry thought as he panted up the mountain ridge, fanning himself with his topee. Everywhere he looked, the ground was criss-crossed with elephant trails and dotted with piles of elephant dung. There must be hundreds of pachyderms in this jungle.

"Pachyderms." Harry spoke the word aloud, relishing every syllable. He loved words. He loved languages. That was one reason why he became so proficient in Burmese. He had lapped up his language lessons like a cat drinking cream. Now he translated Scripture portions for the people who could read. In some dialects where there was no written language, he had to assemble an alphabet and compile a simple dictionary before he could begin.

It was brain-wearying work and Harry was glad that it did not occupy all his time. He preferred to tramp through the villages on preaching tours, telling people about Jesus and distributing books and gospel tracts.

This particular afternoon he was on his way to Nolda village. It was not his first visit, and he knew how many hours the walk took. Today various things had delayed his departure, and no matter how fast he walked he doubted that he would reach the safety of the village before darkness overtook him.

Whistling softly to himself, Harry picked his way over fallen logs and tangled vines, making enough noise to warn the tiny creatures underfoot of his approach.

He hiked for two or three hours, reveling in the quiet beauty of the jungle. During the midafternoon heat, most of the jungle inhabitants enjoyed a siesta, but when evening shadows lengthened they prowled abroad in search of food, and Harry knew what could happen if one of the big cats mistook him for a deer.

Descending the ridge, he followed an overgrown path between mighty teak trees with trunks three or four feet in diameter and broad leaves that looked as large as umbrellas. Here and there immense clumps of bamboos pushed their branchless stems sixty to a hundred feet upward in their search for sunlight. Sometimes the stems of this giant tropical grass measured eight to ten inches thick. The natives put the hollow sections to all sorts of household uses.

They make fine buckets, Harry mused, and cups and house posts and flooring. In fact, he decided, bamboos are as indispensable to the Burmese as coconut palms are to the Indians.

Passing a patch of sensitive mimosa he couldn't resist stopping to boyishly poke the leaves and watch them close up at his touch. He thought, That must be why the Burmese call it *hti-ka-yon* because it opens and closes like an umbrella *(hti)*.

A soft breeze cooling his sweaty face warned Harry that he would not be clear of the jungle before nightfall. I'll have to find somewhere to camp for the night, he thought, then laughed to himself. The very idea of camping, in a literal sense, of trying to pitch a tent in this dense undergrowth was ridiculous. And even if he cleared a space for a tent, an elephant might step on it during the night or a tiger tear it to pieces with teeth and claws. No, *camp* simply meant he'd have to find some safe place to spend the night.

As rapidly as possible, Harry pushed his way toward the dry riverbed, where he would be safer from attack. There the leafy trees, almost meeting overhead, cast a premature gloom, and he stumbled through the sand and patches of water-worn stones in his haste to find a refuge before darkness fell.

Rounding a bend in the dry stream, he pulled up short. What was going on here? The sand had been churned and pitted into deep holes. One here, another there, and there. It looked as if someone had begun mining operations.

Harry dropped to his knees to examine the holes more closely in the fading light. No human being had made them. The shallow pits had been dug by elephants in their search for water. Cautiously, he rose and circled the largest pit, noting the dark patches of wet sand in the bottom of it. The herd had dug deeply and probably would return each night to drink. Where could he go?

A huge banyan tree grew on the nearer bank. Its thick main branch stretched like a cantilever bridge eighteen to twenty feet above the sand. Harry looked at it and nodded his satisfaction. That would be a fine place to hide.

Quickly he took off his heavy boots and jammed them between conveniently protruding roots. Tying his rifle securely to a small branch above his head, he shinnied up the tree and crawled as far out as he could onto the great limb. He made himself comfortable in a part where the limb forked, and fastened his legs to the branch with the length of rope that he always carried for use in emergency.

He had hardly finished when he heard the distant crack of bamboos, rending the quiet air like rifle shots. The feeding elephants were moving toward the riverbed for their evening drink.

No wonder some people call them the lords of the jungle, Harry mused. They're so big that they know they don't have to be afraid of anything. I've never heard such noisy eaters anywhere. There must be a dozen or more of them thrashing around in there. I can hear their bellies rumbling like a thunderstorm.

The noise came closer and louder, and Harry's straining eyes glimpsed the movements of dark bodies among the trees on the farther side of the stream.

By now the light of the full moon was shining into the clearing around the riverbed. A large bull emerged into the light, his uplifted trunk snaking right and left, testing the air. In single file, like animals coming out of Noah's ark, the rest of the herd followed, each one pausing on the bank with raised trunk waving back and forth, testing the warm night air for alien scent.

Harry shrank into his leafy bower, marveling that they did not catch his scent, even if they could not see him. In the bright moonlight he could see them almost as clearly as if it were day.

The last elephant in the line loitering near the bamboos on the bank was a big old cow with a baby at her side. Harry watched her stretching her trunk as high as she could up a tall stalk, pulling and tugging at it until its resilience gave, and the hollow stem split with a resounding crack. With a satisfied stomp of her huge front foot she held the stalk down and curled the tip of her trunk around the bunch of feathery leaves at the top, tearing them off and carrying them to her mouth. Her restless trunk snuffed and sifted through the other leaves, searching for the tender tidbits and tossing the rest aside.

"Fastidious feeders, you lot," Harry grunted. He was so hungry that he felt like devouring soft leaves himself, and he resented the elephant's wanton waste. Then he realized that they were actually doing small animals a service. Wild oxen and deer would come along later and eat the rest of the leaves, food that they could never have reached for themselves.

Using their huge legs as shovels, the elephants set about widening and deepening their water holes. Clearing out loose sand with their vacuum-cleaner trunks, and restlessly swaying about, twitching their ears and tails, they waited for water to fill their soaks.

After all had satisfied their thirst with trunkful after trunkful of cool water, they began to bathe. Stepping down into the holes, they splashed themselves with a spray of diamond drops that glistened in the moonlight. Harry sat entranced. The animals were so close that if he slid forward and stretched his legs down, he could touch the heads of some of them.

He was most attracted by the antics of the cow and her calf. Like all young things, the baby was more interested in playing than in eating or drinking. As he gamboled around on the sand, his doting mother watched him closely, every movement of her huge body portraying her pride and concern. After she had finished her own toilet, she seemed to think that her son should learn to act in an adult manner.

Gently urging him forward with her trunk, she tried to coax the little fellow down into the water hole to drink. But he preferred to play and dug his little legs into the sand, refusing to go near the soak. Again and again she tried the gentle approach. The little fellow would not budge. Then mamma tried sterner measures. Giving him a hard spank with her trunk, she pushed him to the brink of the waterhole.

Either the baby's pride or his hide was hurt, because he squalled in protest, and his mother gave him another none-too-gentle push that sent him sliding feet first down the sandy slope into the water. Still squalling the aggrieved youngster dipped his miniature trunk into the water and pretended to drink.

Occasionally the elephants paused to raise their trunks high and snuff the air, alert for any scent of danger. At these times, Harry held his breath, wondering again why they had not smelled him. Once he had a bad moment when a half-grown bull meandering around the base of the banyan tree found his heavy boots wedged between the roots. The bull explored the boots with his trunk and trumpeted a high, warning note, but the rest of the herd ignored him, and Harry grinned to himself. Perhaps they knew that this young bull was like the boy who cried "Wolf!"

The moon climbed higher and Harry guessed it must have been almost midnight before the elephants decided to move back into the jungle, feeding as they went. He easily estimated their progress by the noise that they made. He judged that they were about fifty yards from his tree when suddenly all fell silent.

Harry's heart seemed to stop and then accelerate its pounding. He knew what that deathly silence meant. The great animals had scented danger. Now they were standing still as statues, silently snuffing the air with their trunks, straining into the darkness for any indication of a predator's whereabouts.

Harry strained too. Every sense alert, he clung to his perch, peering uselessly through the leaves in the direction of the last crashing bamboo. Minutes crawled by. The silence was as suffocating as a blanket thrown over his head. What death-dealing drama was being enacted in the jungle theater?

Harry's violent start could have spilled him from the tree when the baby elephant's piercing shriek, followed by tiger growls, shattered the silence. The entire jungle seemed to erupt into sound; elephants stamping, trumpeting, thrashing madly around, snapping trees and branches in their wild stampede, the tiger spitting, roaring, growling. The noise was enough to turn the bravest heart to water, and Harry felt goose pimples breaking out all over his body as he mentally followed the battle.

Evidently a tiger stalking the elephant herd had seized the little one, and the rest had joined the bereaved mother in chasing the bold marauder. For a wild moment, Harry thought of grabbing his rifle and going to the baby's rescue, but he would be too late to save the little creature's life. Besides, in the dark he might do more harm than good if he happened to injure any of the animals.

Presently the noise of battle died away, to be gradually replaced by the distant sounds of feeding as the herd wandered farther and farther from the banyan tree. For the remainder of the night Harry had a hard time keeping awake, but he dare not sleep lest he slip out of the tree and hurt himself or fall prey to some stray predator.

Swarms of mosquitoes hummed around him, viciously attacking every centimeter of exposed skin and joyfully calling their fellows to the feast. Toward morning it grew cooler, and Harry shivered as the dew congealed in heavy droplets on his clothes and added to his misery. As soon as it was light enough to see, he clambered stiffly down and put on his boots.

Teeth chattering and chilled to the bone, Harry held his rifle at the ready and crept through the trees toward the spot where he expected to find the baby elephant's remains. There were plenty of signs of battle. Flattened bushes, broken trees, and churned up earth, but not a splinter of bone, not a shred of flesh, not a drop of blood. Puzzled, Harry searched the area more carefully, pulling the branches aside, overturning sticks and stones, scuffing the dirt with his boot.

Suddenly, the true scene dawned on him and he laughed in delight. That loyal band of elephants had proved too much for the tiger. Their united efforts had succeeded in driving him off without his supper.

In great good humor Harry set off to trek the miles that remained between him and shelter, breakfast, and sleep.

WHO'S KING OF BEASTS?

7 HARRY'S ADVENTUROUS hike through Elephant Jungle was only weeks behind him when he heard complaints about an elephant on the rampage.

One afternoon a loud clearing of the throat indicated that someone was waiting at his back door and Harry went out to find Kothar-byaw, the headman of Wethpyu-ue village, standing there. As soon as greetings were over, Kothar-byaw launched into his request.

"Thakin, every night an elephant comes and breaks down my banana plants. He eats the fruit and the young, tender leaves and tramples the rest into the ground. Soon I'll have nothing left."

"Where is your plantation, Kothar-byaw?"

"That's just the trouble, Thakin. I have the misfortune to own land on the outskirts of the village, right beside the stream. And each night the elephant comes to drink and then he sees my banana plants so handy to him, he eats and tramples. Alas for me!"

"Is it only one elephant, not a herd?"

"Yes, Thakin, only one elephant. I wish you would kill him."

A lone elephant. Harry's mind immediately leapt to a rogue elephant, an elephant usually ostracized by the rest of the herd. Could this be the one that the government was after? He must find out, and to do so he must get close enough to the animal to see whether the tip of his tusk was broken. The rogue bull had broken a tusk, probably in a long-ago battle with younger bulls.

"I'd like to see him, Kothar-byaw. About what time does he come?"

"Not long after sunset, Thakin. And he tramples the banana plants, and soon I'll be a poor man if you don't do something."

"Yes, yes." Harry nodded. "The moon rises about sundown tonight. Do you think I'd see him if I came to your plantation tonight?"

"Of course, Thakin. He comes every night. Be there before the sun sets, and I will take you and show you the damage he has done."

Despite his good intentions, several things happened to delay Harry, and the sun's last rays were fading behind the treetops when he panted up to Kothar-byaw's bamboo house.

Kothar-byaw was waiting for him at the foot of the ladder, anxiety etching deep lines in his leathery face. "Hurry, Thakin. He will come at any moment."

With Kothar-byaw leading the way, the two hastened down the deserted streets. In villages so close to the jungle no one ventured outside after nightfall. Cows and buffaloes were herded into thornbush-fenced enclosures, and goats and sheep were protected by stout bamboo pens. Even the dogs shared the humble dwellings of their masters, for leopards regularly prowled the streets in search of their favorite food.

Subdued voices and splinters of candlelight piercing the gathering gloom betrayed the villagers' presence, but once past the last hut, the grayness and silence closed around the two men, shutting them into another world, a primitive place where the law of the jungle—the law of tooth and claw—reigned supreme.

It was a clear, warm night, and the moon would soon be high enough to see by. Harry shook off the scary feeling that enveloped him when Kothar-byaw grabbed his arm and announced hoarsely, "This is it."

In front of them, the silhouettes of four huge mango

trees standing in a straight line, thirty or forty feet apart, led from the beginning of Kothar-byaw's plantation down to the farthest point near the stream. Guided by Kothar-byaw's whisperings, Harry shinnied up the thick trunk of the first tree and hid among the leaves.

Scarcely had Kothar-byaw's shadowy form melted into the dusk on his way back to the safety of his house than a faint gurgling and splashing advertised the elephant's arrival. For what seemed like an hour, Harry listened to him drinking and showering trunkfuls of water over his broad back. Then there was silence, and Harry pictured the animal wading across the small stream and climbing the bank, heading straight for Kothar-byaw's bananas. He could not see through the thick curtain of leaves, but a moment later the distinct scrunch of sap-filled banana trunks being torn out of the ground told him that he was correct.

Harry twisted and turned, climbed quietly to a higher branch and burrowed deeper into the leafy screen, but still he could not see the animal. The moonlight was bright enough, but he was too far away.

I'll never see him from this distance. I wonder if I climbed down and ran to the next tree, whether I could see him from there? For a minute or two Harry weighed the matter. Elephants move surprisingly fast, but this one must be nearly a hundred yards away. Surely I could reach the next tree before he reached me.

Finally Harry decided to take the risk, and moving as quietly as he could, he slid down the thick trunk and raced to the next tree. The elephant stopped chewing, and Harry knew that it had heard him running and was listening. But it was a still night and there was no breeze to waft his scent. Presently the scrunching sounds began again.

Harry climbed as far as he dared into the high branches of the mango tree and parted the leaves this way and that, but still he could not see.

"Botheration!" he muttered to himself. The banana plants were confined to the lower part of the garden; there was nothing to lure the elephant up his way. If he wanted to see, he would have to go to the elephant.

I wonder, do I dare? Once again, Harry perched on a branch and debated the pros and cons of changing his position. The third tree was only thirty yards away, its dark leaves beckoned him in the moonlight. Surely if he was *very* careful——

Again he decided to risk it. He slid noiselessly out of the tree and began to move toward the third mango tree. His brain throbbed with fear at the peril of his situation, and his heart pounded so loudly that he felt sure the animal would hear it. Should he forget about noise and make a quick dash for safety or should he act cautiously? The elephant stopped chewing, and Harry knew it was listening intently, so he stood stone-still until he heard the scrunch and squelch of succulent banana leaves again. Then he darted forward.

But the elephant's quick ears heard his movement, and once more the chewing stopped. And once more Harry stood like a poised statue, ready to run for his life if the elephant moved in his direction. Again the animal resumed feeding, and again Harry darted toward the third tree.

To his agonizing mind it seemed to take hours to cover the thirty yards to the next tree. Just as he reached the foot of it the elephant saw him.

With a desperate effort Harry leaped for the lowest branch and swung himself into the tree, climbing rapidly upward until the leaves hid him from view. But the elephant knew now that he was there, and Harry wondered what the next move would be.

Carefully pulling the leaves aside, he peered through. At least he had a perfect view of the elephant now. It stood perfectly still staring at the tree. Elephants have poor eyesight, and perhaps it was trying to decide what kind of beast had disappeared into the mango tree.

All around the animal was clear space where its frequent forays had uprooted Kothar-byaw's banana plants, and the moon shone like a spotlight illumining the scene. Seconds ticked by, and Harry's suspense mounted. Would the elephant attack? Was it preparing to tear down the tree, branch by branch? He knew that he would stand no chance against that reaching, probing trunk. It would fling him to

Heart-stopping seconds went by as Harry wondered whether the elephant had detected him and would attack.

the ground and the great feet would trample him into pulp.

Still the elephant made no move, and Harry's taut nerves were stretched to the breaking point when suddenly a tiger stepped into the small clearing. Silent as an apparition, it appeared and confronted the elephant.

Harry breathed a prayer of gratitude. Now the elephant's attention was diverted from him, and he might witness something interesting. Many times he had listened to hunters, both European and Burmese, arguing about which animal was lord of the jungle. Some said the elephants ruled the jungle and cited instances to prove it. Others were just as positive that the tigers were lords of the jungle and told stories that proved their point. Now he would see for himself which side was correct.

Which one would attack? Which one would give ground?

Suspense swelled into a tangible something that not only Harry felt. Not a leaf stirred, not a frog croaked, the mosquitoes ceased their maddening hum. The whole jungle held its breath as the two motionless, kingly creatures stared at each other.

Suddenly the great elephant panicked. Screaming like a frightened child, he circled madly around the small clearing seeking escape from those bared fangs. Blindly he collided with the fourth mango tree, ricocheted back into the banana plants, and finally bolted across the stream and into the jungle, thrusting bushes and bamboos aside in his mad flight.

For a long time Harry listened to him crashing through the jungle, his uphill progress marked by sounds of cracking and splitting and terrified trumpetings. Harry was not even certain that the tiger had followed the craven creature. When he looked down at the clearing, the pool of moonlight was empty, and he might have convinced himself that he had imagined the entire episode if it was not for the fast-fading sounds of the elephant's flight.

But now what was he to do? Even though the elephant was gone, the tiger might still be somewhere about, perhaps crouched in the shadows licking its paws and purring in feline glee.

Harry felt that he had taken enough risks for one night. It would be risking his life to try and get back to Kothar-byaw's house. He would have to spend the night in the mango tree.

Taking from his pocket, the piece of cord he always carried, he tied his gun to a stout branch. Feeling around among the branches, testing first this fork and then that, he finally wedged his body between the trunk and a thick branch and spent the rest of the uncomfortable night dozing in his leafy bower.

As soon as it was light, Harry clambered stiffly from the tree and trudged through the wet grass to the headman's house. Kothar-byaw and the rest of the villagers had listened, trembling behind barred doors, to the commotion of the previous night, and when Harry told them what he saw in the pool of moonlight, they were as eager as he to know the rest of the story.

Had the tiger chased the elephant when it ran off? Had it caught him? Had there been a fight in the end? They all wanted to go into the jungle with him and find out, but Harry insisted that only Kothar-byaw come. He did not want the responsibility of protecting more than one un-armed villager.

A blind man could have followed that cowardly ele-phant's trail. Torn branches, uprooted bushes, and over-turned rocks littered the jungle, and when Harry and Kothar-byaw panted to the crest of the hill, deep skid marks down the other side showed that the panic-stricken elephant had plumped onto his giant rump and skidded down into the valley.

Harry's imagination pictured the scene, and he laughed until the tears came. "What a tale he'll tell when he rejoins the herd," he chuckled to Kothar-byaw. And to himself he reflected that likely as not there was no such creature as a king of the jungle. Animals are like people, he decided. In any species or race, some are brave, and some are fearful, and one isolated incident can't be made to prove a point.

"There's only one thing I'm sure of, Kothar-byaw," Harry told the chief. "The elephant who ruined your banana plants is not the wanted rogue. I saw his tusks plainly in the moonlight, and they were whole, beautiful ivories."

A CHALLENGE FOR HARRY

8 "IT WILL be a very responsible position——"
"But he has all the necessary qualifications."
Distribution of labor was under discussion at the
constituency meeting in Rangoon. Elder W. A.
Spicer, General Conference president, was present,
and it was he who suggested that Harry Skinner be asked to
go into the wild Shan State and open up the Seventh-day
Adventist work there.

More than one hundred tribes lived in the state. They
spoke different dialects, some so unrelated that tribes living
in one district could not converse with people living only a
handful of miles away.

"Now, there's a challenge for you, Harry, m'boy," Harry
said to himself when he heard of the appointment. "You'll
be a *real* pioneer this time."

The Burmese railway had pushed only as far as Heho,
across the valley from Taunggyi ("big mountain"), the
government and military headquarters for the district.
Perched on a 5,000-foot plateau, a thousand miles from
steamy Rangoon, Taunggyi had a pleasant climate, and
Harry decided to make his home there. He rented a house
large enough to serve as office, clinic, school, or whatever
else might be needed, and began his work for the Taungthu
people.

He spent the first few weeks meeting government officials and as many of the local dignitaries and military men
as possible.

"Now I must visit around and become acquainted with the *sawbwas* ["chiefs"]," Harry told himself. "I must learn the language of the people and study their customs."

Sometimes on foot, sometimes in lumbering bullock carts, Harry sought out the primitive villagers. In an amazingly short time he picked up a working knowledge of their languages and customs.

One afternoon, Harry tramped into an isolated jumble of huts, glorified by the title of village, and sought out the chief. They exchanged the customary greetings, and the chief invited Harry into his hut.

Harry stepped forward, and the smile on his face froze. A necklace of mummified human heads hung across the doorway, their black hair dangling down like a curtain.

The chief carelessly brushed the hair aside and entered, but Harry had no relish for dead men's locks tickling the back of his neck. He stooped low and half-crawled into the hut.

The two of them sat on woven grass mats, and Harry answered all the usual questions as to who he was and why he was here and what he intended doing, but he was consumed with curiosity and itching to ask a few questions himself. Gradually he steered the conversation around to the hut's strange decoration.

"What is the significance of this—ah—these heads across your doorway?"

Expressions of pride and regret fought for precedence on the old chief's wrinkled face.

"Times are changing, Thakin. When I was a youth, the young men of our tribe were not permitted to marry until we had proved our manhood by slaying some of our enemies."

"How many did you have to kill?"

"About seven or eight, Thakin. If there were no convenient tribal battles raging, we lay in wait beside jungle paths."

"Did you, ah—ah—did you eat your victims?"

"Oh, no, Thakin!" The old man sounded righteously indignant. "We did not eat them. We cut off their heads and pickled them in a preservative made from a certain tree bark. When they had soaked a long time, we dried them out and threaded them on string so . . . " He waved toward the fringe of hair falling across his doorway.

"Very interesting."

Harry took his leave of the old man and walked through the village. Hut after hut wore similar bizarre embellishments. Shans still bore a reputation for being fierce, bloodthirsty people, Harry thought. Who knew what young buck, with nostalgic longings for the old ways, might be stealthily seeking to prove his manhood? Harry decided he wasn't going to linger in that village.

A LEOPARD IN THE LIVING ROOM

9 HARRY'S TABLE, doubling as a desk, never seemed to be large enough for all the books and papers that accumulated on it. In the middle were piles of mission reports that had to be filled out in duplicate or triplicate and sent to various departments. Pompous, ambiguous government circulars that required careful attention lest the wrath of officialdom be incurred, occupied one end. Letters and newspapers from home overflowed onto a nearby chair. Stacks of books and dictionaries needed for his translation work balanced on the other end, together with reams of lined foolscap, weighted down with the hammer that Harry left there when he knocked down a nail in his boot.

A woman's hands would have itched to tidy everything up and set the place to rights, but Harry was proud of his establishment and liked everything just as it was. With no one else around, he claimed that he could put a thing down and know exactly where to find it next time he wanted it.

Nevertheless, despite all his assertions that he did not mind being alone, he threw his topee into the air and yelled with glee when he learned of Ben Brown's* appointment to the Shan territory. It would be great to have someone to work with him, even if for only a few months.

"What a time we'll have together," Harry chortled to the heavy old table as he set two chairs, one on either side of it.

---

* Not his real name

"I'll have to clear some of this junk off you, so that Ben'll have a place to sit. I hope he brings some of his goods in decent-sized packing cases. We could use another one or two—put shelves in them and make cupboards for the kitchen gear.

"I'll have to get a bed for him too." Even though he was quite alone, Harry could not keep the delighted grin off his face as he tidied up his house in preparation for Ben's arrival. "I'd better get the local carpenter working on that straight away. He's so slow. Probably need a few more chairs, too, in case we have visitors."

Their fellowship was all that Harry anticipated. Ben was a likable, fun-loving young man, and the two of them got on well together. They shared the work between them, divided the living expenses, and in general enjoyed each other's company.

Some weeks after Ben's arrival, urgent mission needs necessitated a trip to Rangoon, and Harry generously arranged for his friend to go.

"I'm more accustomed to the solitude up here, Ben, and I can speak the lingo better—although you're coming along fine. You go. But hurry back," he added with a touch of wistfulness.

Two weeks crawled by. Ben should be returning any day now. If he did not get back soon, he'd be in trouble. Already violent thunderstorms rumbling through the mountains heralded the approach of an early monsoon. Once the rains came, travel would be nearly impossible. Landslides and swollen rivers could cause indefinite delays.

Harry worried about Ben, and every day he asked his servants and neighbors whether they knew anything about the conditions of the road. There was no local telephone or telegraph service by which he could keep in touch, but the native people had that indefinable something known as bush wireless, a mysterious method whereby they sensed news, particularly bad news, long before white people were aware of it.

No, they knew nothing, and all that Harry could do was to hope and pray that Ben would arrive back safely.

One particular day the rain pelted down so hard that Harry could not work outside. He spent most of the time sitting at the table, busy with his translation work, although he interrupted it a dozen times to go to the door and look down the trail, hoping for a glimpse of Ben returning.

When evening came Harry lighted the lamp and sat at the table, head propped in hands, reading a volume of the *Testimonies*. He managed to concentrate in spite of the wild rain lashing the trees outside and the persistent plop, plop inside the house, as leaks from the thatched roof dripped into strategically placed buckets and basins. Once or twice he interrupted his reading to stare out into the darkness and pray for Ben's safety, wherever he might be. In such weather, who knew when he would come.

An hour passed. Harry moved only when he turned a page. No disturbing noises drifted from the nearby village where men and animals huddled into whatever shelter they could find and waited out the storm. No breeze wafted through the open door leading onto the veranda behind him.

Presently the rain, and then the monotonous *plop-plop-ping*, ceased, but Harry did not notice anything until a faint scraping sound penetrated his absorption. Without moving he became suddenly alert, listening intently. He heard it again. A soft sound, like a light footfall.

It's Ben. Harry smiled to himself. He's arrived back, and he thinks he's going to sneak up on me and give me a surprise. Well, I won't spoil his little joke. I'll let him come. He deserves some fun after the miserable journey he must have had.

Stifling his chuckles and keeping perfectly still, Harry listened to the faint, steady footfalls coming closer. Then the merest creak of bamboo flooring. Ben must be right behind his chair now. In a moment he'd grab him by the shoulders and yell, "Surprise!"

Harry's grin broadened. He tensed himself for his friend's spring. Instead, a nerve-shattering *thump, bump, bang* made him jump. His heart missed a beat. That was not Ben. Something had bumped into the big wooden box that stood out from the wall between him and the door.

Harry whirled around in time to see a large leopard slinking toward the veranda door.

Gasping, Harry looked wildly around for a weapon. The leopard would be gone before he could reach the gunrack on the wall. His eye fell on the hammer. Seizing it, he threw it with all his might.

The hammer crashed against the wall and the startled leopard leaped through the doorway and disappeared into the darkness.

In one bound Harry reached the door and banged it shut. Panting with fright, he leaned against the doorpost and tried to reconstruct what had gone on behind his back. The leopard's muddy footprints led from the door almost up to his chair and back again. The animal must have nearly breathed down the back of his neck!

Harry shivered at the thought of what might have been. Apparently, the fact that he sat so still saved him from attack. And when the leopard scented its natural enemy, man, it decided to leave and bumped into the wooden box on the way out.

Again Harry shuddered. What if the animal had been a man-eater? He knew the answer. He had heard many tales of the audacity of man-hungry carnivore.

Then why had the leopard come so boldly right into his house? Light usually scares wild animals away. Oohnine and other hunters wise in jungle lore had advised him always to carry a lantern or keep a fire going all night if he had to camp in the jungle.

Harry could not answer the question. Perhaps the leopard was young and inexperienced. Or perhaps it was unnaturally curious.

Whatever may have been the reason for the visit, he was thankful he had missed the animal with his hammer throw. Wild animals do not usually retreat when attacked; they retaliate.

Harry bowed his head in a prayer of gratitude to God for keeping him safe. Then he went back to the table to resume his reading, thinking What a tale I'll have to tell Ben when he returns. This is one he won't believe.

And he was right. When Ben arrived safely the next day he had to trace for himself the leopard's footprints from door to chair and back again, before he would be convinced that Harry had not dreamed the whole experience.

You never can tell when—or where—you may meet a leopard in the Shan hills.

OLD OVERCOMER

10 STRANGERS MUST have wondered about the friendship between Harry and Oohnine (Old Overcomer). The old Shan hunter was weatherbeaten and stooped, his bronze skin wrinkled and toughened from years of exposure. Harry was young and straight and fair. On the surface it seemed that the two had nothing in common except the Burmese language, which Harry spoke like a native. But between them existed a warm bond of understanding that went deeper than any differences of race and religion.

On sunny days the ragged old hunter sometimes slipped silently up to the doorway, through which he could see Harry's head bent over a pile of books and papers, and coughed discreetly. Then Harry grinned, turned in his chair and called, "All right, Oohnine. I'll be there in a little while. I have to finish translating this chapter before I can go anywhere."

The old hunter did not mind waiting. He squatted in the dusty patch of shade beside the door, leaned his back against the wall, and clasped his gnarled hands around his bony knees.

On this particular day the translation took more than an hour to complete, and old Oohnine nodded and dozed in the cool shade, springing to sudden life when he heard the scrape of Harry's chair and the faint click of the rifle being lifted down from its rack.

"Come on now, let's go." Harry jammed his topee on his head, and the two set off as delighted as schoolboys escaping from the drudgery of books and exams.

It was during these long walks together that Harry learned much of his jungle lore. Old Oohnine read the jungle like Harry read a written language. Every displaced leaf, every faint track crossing the path, every sound, every smell told him something that he imparted to Harry, trying to cram a lifetime's experience into each lesson.

For hours they walked and talked and watched and listened. Toward evening as they trudged back down the hill toward Taunggyi a train puffed importantly into the little mountain station. The sparks flying from its wood-burning engine seemed to kindle Oohnine's memory, and he slowed to a stop, his old eyes bright with reminiscences, and his right hand gently fingering the deep scars on his left arm.

Harry had often seen the scars when the old man's tattered sleeve failed to cover the ugly marks, and he had meant to ask Oohnine about them someday, but when the two were together there was so much to say, so much to learn, that he forgot.

Now Oohnine sank to his haunches, his eyes still on the train, and Harry flopped down on the grass beside him, loath to intrude on the old man's memories.

"I lived here when the railway line was built." Oohnine still ran his fingers along the deep scars that scored his arm and shoulder. "I watched the coolies, mostly Indians, dig out the soil and carry it away in baskets on their heads. I saw them put the heavy ties in position and lay the tracks. And the day that the railway opened everyone for miles around came in for the celebrations. There were bands and flags, and all the British government officials and the Burmese officials made speeches and congratulated one another. What a day it was!

"As I watched the first train chug triumphantly up the steep mountainside I wondered what kind of animals the British Government had imprisoned in that black iron cage—animals so strong that they could pull that monstrous creation up the mountains."

Harry chuckled softly. The train was a tiny, two-foot gauge, little more than a toy in his estimation.

Oohnine ignored his mirth and went on. "The trains fascinated me, and whenever I could I went to watch the strange thing pull up at the station and vomit many people out of its long red belly.

"Early one afternoon I was squatting away up at one end of the platform, watching, when the train pulled in, and I saw a thakin step out and walk up to the station agent, who spoke English quite well.

"The thakin was a splendid figure in military uniform, all braid and brass buttons, and he had a big pile of luggage, and a servant with him to carry it, and another servant with a wide red belt, so everyone knew he was an Indian cook-bearer. Quite a dazzling outfit for our little siding, and I wondered why they'd come. After the thakin had talked a little while, the station agent called out to me, 'Eh, Oohnine.'

"I went over to see what he wanted, and he spoke to me in Shan language, 'This thakin is on leave from the army, and he's come up here to do some hunting and shooting. He says he wants to shoot a bear.'

"'Does he know anything about the ways of bears?'

"'I've already asked him that, and he says he does.'

"'Ask him again,' I said. 'Bears are extremely dangerous animals and this thakin does not look to me as though as he knows much about the ways of any kind of animals.'

"The thakin had a gun, Harry. Oh, what a gun! How I would have loved to possess a gun like that.

"So the station agent and the army officer talked together for a while and then the station agent said to me, 'Yes, he says he knows all about bears, and he wants to shoot one. I told him he was lucky to find you here, because you are the finest hunter in the Shan State, so he wants you to go with him, and he will pay you.'

"'Tell the thakin he is in luck,' I said. 'If he wants a bear to shoot, I know there is a she-bear with two cubs living in a thicket over there.' I pointed out the place not far from where we are sitting now, Harry, only it had very many

Oohnine was astonished to see the brave thakin rushing in terror down the path.

more trees and bushes on it then.

"The thakin was delighted. He dumped all his gear on the platform, left his servants to mind it, and he took his beautiful gun and some cartridges and we set off. I had my *dah-shey*."

Harry nodded. Of course Oohnine carried his *dah-shey*. No Shan man went anywhere without that all-purpose knife, so heavy that it needed both hands to wield it and so long that it could not be stuck in the wearer's belt like an ordinary knife, but had to be carried over the shoulder lest it trip up its owner.

"We did not understand a single word of each other's language, but we made signs. I pointed out to him exactly where the bear was and which way she was likely to come. He nodded and raised his rifle to show me that he was all ready for her attack. We made no effort to be quiet because we wanted the she-bear to come out after us.

"We were only about fifty paces from her hiding place
when that shaggy black bear heard us and bounced out of
cover like a huge rubber ball and came toward us, growling
and snorting and working herself up into a terrible rage.
Bears are a bad-tempered lot at any time, and a she-bear
with young is something to be feared. But I was not afraid,
not with the thakin and his wonderful gun beside me. I
knew he could shoot that bear at fifty paces as easily as I
could swat a fly.

"I watched the bear come nearer, frothing and fuming,
and any moment I expected to hear the crack of his rifle, but
nothing happened. I hated to take my eyes off her, but she
was getting too close for safety now, he should fire at once. I
yelled, but still no shot, so I turned round to signal to the
thakin to shoot quickly—and he was not there! He was not
beside me anymore. I was mystified. Where had he gone?

"Then I looked behind, and there was the thakin running
for his life toward the station. I stared after him, too
surprised to remember the danger I was in. A thakin running! A brave white man running away from a bear! If
anyone had told me that, I would not have believed him.

"A sudden spirit of bravado rushed into me. I had no gun
but I'd show that craven white man what a brave Shan could
do. I'd cleave that she-bear's head right in half with my
dah-shey. I grasped the heavy knife with both hands and
raised it high above my head. The bear was almost upon me,
screaming with fury and shaking her head wildly from side
to side as she combed the air with her murderous claws.

"I brought my dah-shey down on her skull with force
enough to smash an iron bar, but at that very instant she
shook her head, and the knife slipped off her wiry black hair
without inflicting the slightest wound.

"Instantly she was upon me, biting and tearing at my
arm with her teeth; ripping my body with her claws. I yelled
and twisted and tried to fight her off but she held on, strong
as twenty men, chewing my biceps muscle with her yellow
teeth and shredding my flesh. I shrieked in agony, and
struggled and fought, but all I could move was my elbow,

which was pressed into her stomach as she held me to her. Desperately I thumped her middle with not a hope of hurting her. But it must have tickled, because she relaxed ever so slightly and I wrenched myself free and ran as I have never run before, leaving a trail of blood behind me all the way to the station, where the thakin in his gorgeous uniform, and holding his beautiful gun, stood trembling, watching me come.

"The station agent got out his first-aid kit and stopped the blood and bound up my wounds. He told me, later, that he did not expect me to live, and neither did the thakin. My arm and shoulder were torn to pieces. Even if they healed, he said, blood poisoning usually sets in."

"Did the army officer take you down to the city to the hospital?"

"No, Harry Thakin. He gave me some money, and that was the end of the matter as far as he was concerned. He expected me to die."

"It's a wonder that you didn't!" Harry gasped when Oohnine pulled his shirt open and showed the full extent of his scars. His chest and back were ridged and puckered. His arm and shoulder furrowed and misshapen.

Harry shook his head. "I don't know how you escaped infection. Bear's claws are always filthy."

"The time of my death had not yet come. I could not die," the old man replied, his solemn eyes resting on his young companion.

BLUFFING A TIGER

11 WOULD YOU be able to accommodate the Wyman family for a month or so? Rangoon is hot now so they are eager to take their leave in the hills. Perhaps you would have time to assist Brother Wyman with his language study while they are there."

Harry felt like leaping into the air and shouting "Whoopee!" as he laid the letter from the mission superintendent on his desk. Frank and Nellie Wyman coming up to stay with him! Nothing could be better. He'd known them in Rangoon. And their little girl, what was her name? Ah, yes, Ruth Alice. It would be wonderful to see them again.

Harry's affirmative reply went by return post, and in the intervening weeks he straightened up his bachelor establishment—nailing a board over the hole where rats had gnawed their way into the kitchen, emptying all his "junk" out of the spare room, fixing the bathroom door so that it shut properly instead of leaving a three-inch-wide gap. He must have everything just so before his company arrived.

My, won't it be great to have someone to talk English with again? he thought. Harry was so used to speaking to the villagers in Shan or Burmese that sometimes he even found himself thinking in a foreign language.

The Wymans' visit was all that Harry hoped it would be. Renewed friendship and the house full of adult talk and childish laughter. Yes, and it was good to see a woman bustling about, made the place seem like a home—even though Mrs. Wyman's presence did keep Harry on his toes, remembering to empty the bath water and pick up his soiled clothes and not leave his books and papers scattered over the dining table.

After the family had been at Taunggyi nearly a week, Harry came into the living room early one morning to find Frank studying, while Nellie and Ruth Alice bargained with a vegetable seller at the back door.

"Do you feel like taking a long walk today, Frank?"

Frank nodded, but before he could speak, Harry continued. "I'm going to Ga-Nine-Shey, about seven miles down the mountain, to visit Maung-Hpo-Yin. He's the most notorious bandit in the district. Missionaries of all denominations have tried to convert him, but he's a tough nut. I've talked to him, too, and the last time I was down that way he said to me, 'Thakin, I want to try your brand of medicine."

"So I've arranged to go down and answer some Bible questions for him, but I warn you, it will be an all-day visit. He and his wife are great talkers, and they are sure to insist that we have a meal with them. You'd better tell Nellie not to expect you home before dark."

"I'll be glad to come." Frank shut his language book with a bang, and Harry laughed. "Oh, you won't get off that easily. All the conversation will be in Burmese, so if you concentrate and try to follow it, that will help you more than any book can."

Frank grimaced and Harry continued, "Wear your topee. It's quite hot at the foot of the mountain, and we'd better take a lantern, some matches, and a length of rope. I never go for any long walk without being prepared for emergencies." Harry buckled a service revolver around his waist as he spoke. "A British army officer used to spend his leaves up here with me, and he gave me this 'howitzer' and made me promise never to go anywhere without it. Jolly thing weighs a ton, but I guess the look of it would scare robbers away."

"What about wild animals?"

"Oh, it wouldn't be much use against a big animal, but it will be full moon tonight, and I don't expect that we'll see anything larger than monkeys or deer."

As soon as breakfast was over, the two men set off. The narrow trail descended the mountain so steeply that in some places they were able to jog along, and within two hours they were climbing the bamboo ladder that led to Maung Hpo-yin's veranda.

The day passed exactly as Harry had predicted. They talked a great deal, studied the Bible, and felt encouraged that the one-time bandit really seemed to have decided to become a Christian. About midafternoon the wife insisted that they must eat before they left. So they all talked some more and waited politely while she kindled a little fire between three stones on the earthen hearth, filled the big clay pot with water, and measured out the rice.

It took a long time for the rice to cook, and the white men coughed and choked, and their eyes filled with tears as the smoke from the cooking fire curled through the one-room house. Maung-Hpo-Yin and his wife did not seem to notice the smoke and spent the time regaling Harry and Frank with all the local news.

"Have you heard about the tiger lurking around the other side of the mountain? It's an old animal. Its teeth and claws are worn down and it can't run fast enough to catch deer anymore, so it has begun killing domestic cattle. Soon it will start on human beings, and then become a man-eater. You see if it doesn't."

"I wonder if that's the same animal that attacked a plowman in broad daylight a few weeks ago?" Harry mused. "He would have been killed if the villagers had not heard his screams and rushed out with sticks and stones and driven the tiger away. They brought the man up to my bungalow. Fortunately, his wounds were not too deep, and I was able to treat them."

"I hope that tiger is content to stay on the other side of the mountain," Frank commented. "I have no desire to meet a man-eater."

The conversation hopped from one topic to another until finally the meal was served and eaten. Then Frank and Harry said their farewells and started on their return journey. Darkness fell while they trudged the two miles of flat country before arriving at the mountain trail. Worse still, a violent windstorm sprang up, and thick clouds scudded across the sky, blotting out the moon. Again and again the men tried to light the kerosene lantern that Frank carried, but as fast as they struck a match, the wind blew it out.

"Let's take off our coats and hold them around the lantern," Frank suggested. "We must have light. That steep path was bad enough in the daylight. I wouldn't like to tackle it in the dark."

Crouching down and shielding the lantern and matches with their coats, the men finally got the wick to light and the glass fastened in place. As they straightened up, a low, ominous growl warned them of danger.

Harry snatched up the lantern and held it high. The beam of light fell on a tiger, squatting catlike on the shadowy path ahead, watching them.

Harry's heart pounded. No ordinary tiger would act like that. This must be the daring animal they'd heard about, the one that attacked the plowman. Sending up a silent prayer for protection, he choked back his fears, and said loudly, "Don't be afraid, Frank. There's only one way to deal with this fellow and that's to bluff him. You carry the lantern and keep close behind me so that the light throws my shadow ahead. I hope that will confuse him some. Don't panic. We must go straight on. If we panic and run, we're dead men."

Striving to walk naturally on their trembling legs, the two started up the mountain trail. Harry held the heavy revolver ready. The big, old weapon could kill a man easily enough, but it was too uncertain to use against a tiger, except in the most dire circumstance.

Step by step, praying as they went, the men advanced, and the tiger continued its rumbling growls. When it saw that the growls failed to stop them, it opened its mouth in deafening roars in an effort to make them panic.

All the time Harry kept up a constant patter of talk, as much to encourage himself as his companion. "Come on, Frank, we can't let this critter get the better of us. Keep close behind me. Hold the lantern high."

Nearer and nearer, and still the tiger stood its ground, snarling and spitting defiance. Harry's heart seemed to stick in his throat, nearly strangling him. Something had to give. They couldn't keep walking until they were on top of the tiger.

Another step, and another. Only a short distance to go when suddenly the great cat, still spitting and snarling, slunk off the path and let them pass.

"Watch out! He'll be back!" Harry panted, and they climbed as fast as they could up the tortuous path. "He won't give up that easily." As if hoping to catch them off guard, the tiger waited around the next bend, but the lantern light picked out his gleaming eyes, and the battle began again.

"Let's trying scaring him away. Throw stones near him, Frank, crash them all around but don't hit him. I don't know what he might do if we hit him."

The men found ready ammunition in the rocks that littered the mountainside. But their barrage of stones only made the animal more furious, and his roaring challenges reverberated from crag to crag.

Nearer and nearer. Would the crazy animal never move? What if this time it stood its ground and sprang at them when they were close enough? Harry's steps nearly faltered, and his silent prayers were frantic in their importunity. Heavenly Father save us! Save us! Drive the tiger away. At any rate save Frank, Father. Nellie and the child need him.

Once more their prayers were answered, and it was the tiger that gave ground as they approached. At the last possible moment he slunk off the path, only to reappear minutes later at a spot far above their heads where the trail wound round the mountain.

Up, up, up the men toiled while the tiger lurked above, hissing and cursing them in tiger talk, and retreating only when collision seemed inevitable.

Again and again the battle of nerves was fought until Frank and Harry thankfully gained the safety of the well-traveled track along the mountain crest. No climb had ever seemed so long, and no home ever looked so good as Harry's humble bungalow did that night.

The next time Harry visited Ga-nine-shey, he told Maung Hpo-yin about the night's adventure.

"I know," the man grinned triumphantly. "From here we heard the tiger screeching, and all the villagers stood in their doorways listening. All those hours we followed your progress up the mountainside, and I told the people, 'Do not worry about them. They will be all right. Payah-Thakin [God] will protect them.'"

OF BULLS AND BANDITS

12 AFTER THE tiger encounter, Harry felt that it would be wise to let a bit of time elapse before suggesting another journey. He knew Frank was ready to tackle any experience, but Nellie and Ruth Alice might not be so happy about having him go trekking through the jungle again.

One morning after breakfast he said, "I have to take some supplies to one of the outstation schools, Frank. It's about sixty miles away, and we'll go by bullock cart. Htee-lun will drive. You know him, the tall fellow from the Pa-oh tribe. He's a brave boy and a good companion on any trip."

"How long will the trip take?" The Wymans' leave was drawing to a close, and Frank did not want to try anything that would delay their return to Rangoon.

"About four days. I have the best pair of bulls in this part of the country." Harry could not resist boasting about his bulls. They were the pride of his heart, and worth a lot of money. "The zebu bull is a placid animal. I can trust him in any situation. The red one is part wild stock and a bit excitable, but they pull well together. Even so," he added candidly, "we average only about two miles an hour, and one never knows what might happen along the way—or be waiting for us when we arrive."

Frank laughed and slapped his knee. "How right you are! But I'll be glad to come with you if it's only four or five days. I'm sure Nellie won't mind."

Nellie did not mind, and very early the next morning, the three men loaded the boxes of slates and chalk and other goods for the school onto the heavy, springless cart, which looked substantial enough to transport an elephant. They piled their own bundles of clothes and bedding on top and carefully stowed the hamper of food Nellie had packed for them, under the driver's seat. Harry and Frank climbed into the back, and Hteelun took his place up front on the solid plank that served as the driver's seat.

It took a great deal of tongue-clucking and coaxing on Hteelun's part to get the bulls moving, but eventually the huge iron-shod wheels turned and the cart rumbled off over the rough road, with Nellie and Ruth Alice calling goodbye and waving until they were out of sight.

Hour after hour the slow-moving animals lumbered along, providing the power that made the cumbersome wooden wheels squeal with each revolution of wooden nave and axle. At close quarters the continuous *squeak, squeal, squeak, squeal,* was like a woman shrieking, but Harry was used to the sound, and it did not bother him. He did agree with Frank that traveling in a springless bullock cart with only a foot-high pile of straw to cushion one's bones, must surely be the most uncomfortable mode of travel in the world.

Sometimes Frank and Harry talked as they went along. Sometimes they read one of the books they had brought with them. But reading was not easy when every little while an extra-savage jolt jerked the books out of their hands and they had to retrieve them and flip through the pages to find the place again.

At nightfall they stopped to feed and water the animals and let them rest while they themselves built a fire and cooked a meal. Once the sun had set, the air was pleasantly cool, and the men sat around the campfire eating and talking about the gospel work yet to be done in the unentered areas of Burma.

"We've come a long way since 1902 when Herbie Myers came over from India to sell Seventh-day Adventist books to the English-speaking population," Frank mused, "but there's still a colossal task ahead of us."

"How are your treatment rooms going, Frank?"

"Really well. Helping people physically breaks down a lot of prejudice. You know we've opened a Telegu church in Rangoon now, don't you? That's besides the English and Burmese churches."

"Yes, I do a lot of translating work for the union, and even though I'm so far away I keep in touch with what's going on. I hope the work goes ahead as fast in the next twenty years as it has during the past twenty."

"Speaking of going ahead, hadn't we better get moving?"

"Yes." Harry nodded and reluctantly unfolded himself. With Hteelun's help, the cart was soon reloaded, and they started off again. The bulls moved so slowly that they seemed to sleep as they went, and Hteelun needed only to wind the reins around his hands to keep them taut, and he too could doze as they meandered along.

Harry rested his back against a box and made himself as comfortable as he could, even though he knew he would be fortunate if he managed the shortest of catnaps in between jolts.

About 3:00 A.M. Harry gave up. His entire body ached, and his stiff muscles rebelled against any further torture. Yawning, he looked around. The half-moon had set about midnight, but the starlight was bright enough to throw the dark shapes of trees and bushes into silhouette against the deep violet sky. The bulls looked gray and ghostly in the predawn twilight. Dew glistened on their shiny hides and curved horns. The slack nose ropes and Hteelun's bobbing head showed that their driver slept.

Frank stirred, groaned, and rubbed his numbed limbs to restore circulation. "Are you awake?" he asked raspily.

"Yes, and I've had about as much of this cart as I can stand." Harry yawned again. "According to my reckoning we must be nearly halfway. Frank, there's enough light to see by. Why don't we get out and walk for a while? We can stride along and straighten out the kinks, and when we get tired we can sit by the side of the road and wait until Hteelun catches up."

"Great idea." Like a pair of stiff-jointed puppets, the two men clambered out of the cart, woke Hteelun, and told him their plan, then set off at a brisk walk.

Soon the creaking bullock cart fell far behind, and apart from their own voices, no sound marred the early morning stillness. For more than two miles they kept up a steady pace, breathing deeply, and enjoying the pure, clean air, free from the dust stirred up by the bulls' plodding hooves.

Around the next bend in the trail they saw a fallen tree conveniently near, and Frank suggested that they rest awhile and wait for the cart.

"We can speak Burmese and get in a bit of study." He rubbed the palms of his hands together. "I must tap that brain of yours as much as I can while we're together, Harry m'boy."

Harry laughed, and while the eastern sky slowly lightened to a pallid blue, the two sat on the log engrossed in Burmese verbs and tenses. Suddenly Frank raised his head:

"What's that noise?"

Both men turned their heads, listening intently to a faint sound in the distance. It grew louder, came nearer, resolved itself into words.

"Thakin Harry. Thakin. Thak——"

"It's Hteelun!" Harry leaped up and bolted back down the road with Frank at his heels. Why was the boy shouting? What could be wrong?

They pounded a quarter mile down the road before they saw Hteelun running toward them. He pulled up when he saw them coming and waited, chest heaving, gasping, almost too breathless to speak coherently. Harry grabbed him by the arm.

"What's happened, Hteelun? Where's the cart?"

"Bandits, Thakin," the boy panted. "I was driving—quietly along—when four bandits—suddenly sprang—out of the bushes alongside the road—and snatched the reins out of my hands. One of them held a knife over my head—while the others unyoked the bulls and drove them off into the bush. Thakin, I didn't know what to do—there were four of them——"

"It's all right, Hteelun," Harry soothed the frightened youth. "You couldn't do anything against so many. They might have killed you. But we must get those bulls back. They only slaughter them for food, and we can't let that happen."

The three hurried back to the abandoned cart, now tipped with its single shaft pointing skywards, and its rear sunk into the dust. Nothing else had been taken. Harry leaned over the side where his personal belongings were stacked and rustled around in the straw until he found the huge elephant rifle that his friend, the forestry officer, loaned him to take on long trips.

Hteelun's eyes gleamed when he saw the big rifle. *"Wet-oo-they-r-nart!* ["The spirit of death gun!"]" he exclaimed. The gun that could kill an animal as large as an elephant at fifty paces. The sight of the weapon seemed to put new courage into him.

Frank rustled around on his side of the cart, pushing the straw this way and that until he unearthed a shotgun. When he saw it Harry's mouth dropped open. "I didn't know you had that with you. Why did you bring it along?"

"Oh, I thought it might come in handy if we ran out of food. I might be able to shoot a couple of ducks or something for the pot."

"Not a bad idea." Harry turned to speak to Hteelun but the youth was feverishly ferreting around in the straw under a box of chalk, and presently he drew out his long *dah-shey.* A mighty weapon—the handle alone was over twelve inches long and needed both hands of a strong man to wield it. Brave as a lion, now that he had the two white men to back him up, Hteelun waved the sword above his head and made ready to deal a mortal blow to any bandit that might appear.

"Which way did the bandits go?" Harry looked at Hteelun, and the boy swung his sword around to all points of the compass: "That way, Thakin, that way."

Harry shrugged, and started to prowl along the side of the road. Dawn's light and the four-feet high grass trampled in one place beside the trail soon answered his question. He leaped forward and then paused to shout over his shoulder: "Frank, you'd better stay at the cart and guard the stuff. Hteelun, you go ahead of me. You can run faster than I can."

It was easy to follow the trail of trampled grass and bushes that gave way to soft dirt showing the bulls' tracks. The two ran steadily for nearly an hour before they came to a large clearing in the jungle. In the center of the clearing stood a solitary hut, built up on tall bamboo piles.

Hteelun was fifty or sixty paces ahead, and Harry heard him shout that he could see the stolen bulls tied to a post under the hut. He waved his sword menacingly above his head and dashed across the open area unmindful of the four bandits that Harry saw lolling on the hut veranda.

The bandits leaped to their feet, cursing and threatening the boy, but making no move to rush down the ladder and overpower him, as they surely would have done if they had not spied Harry with his huge gun break cover and race toward them.

Harry's heart pounded madly, and not only from running. He knew something that none of the others knew— His gun was empty! He had forgotten to load it or bring any ammunition. All the bullets lay hidden under the straw in the back of the cart.

If the bandits suspected that his gun was empty, Harry knew that they would not hesitate to hack him and Hteelun to death, and bury the evidence. Pausing in his advance, he raised his gun, opened the lock, pretended to load, and slammed it shut again with a great show and rattle.

Hteelun rushed under the hut and struggled to undo the knots that the captive bulls had drawn tight in their excited plunging and tossing. Harry continued to run forward. He was halfway across the clearing when the bandit chief suddenly grabbed his swordlike *dah-shey* and sprang down the ladder, making straight toward him.

Harry went cold. What now? Had his bluff failed? He knew that these tribesmen could not only wield an expert sword but they could throw one with deadly accuracy. Was he to be cut down as he ran?

Praying in his heart, Harry kept running forward, and

With his gun empty, Harry faced the bandit chief coming at him, sword in hand.

the advancing bandit suddenly shouted in dialect, "My lord, white man."

Throwing his sword, handle first, in a gesture of surrender, he flung himself at Harry's feet.

Harry almost collapsed with relief, but he assumed a ferocious frown and rushed toward the bandit chief, knocking the man's headband off with his knee. He knew that this was the most degrading treatment that could be meted out to any Burmese, particularly a chief.

"You villain." Harry held his gun to the man's head. "How dare you steal those bulls!"

The chief cowered still lower. "Oh, Thakin, my lord, I didn't know they belonged to a white man or I wouldn't have done it."

"But you did do it." Harry struggled to keep his voice stern. He felt sorry for the poor fellow cringing there in front of him.

"It's lucky for you that those animals belonged to me, a missionary. If I were a government officer, you'd be severely punished. But I am a man of God and I love all men as brothers. Here——" Harry picked up the man's sword and held it out to him.

"No." The chief made no attempt to take it. "I am your slave."

Harry knew what he meant. According to Burmese custom, when two men met in combat the vanquished always became slave of the victor.

"No, no." Still leaving the sword on the ground where the bandit might easily snatch it up and attack him, Harry held out his hand. "Let us be friends. What is your name?"

"They call me Dah-mya ["knife-thrower"]."

"All right, Dah-mya, let us——," and while the three bandits on the veranda gaped and muttered, Harry helped the chief to his feet, and the two of them walked, talking as they went, to the edge of the clearing where Hteelun waited with the bulls.

"Are you married, Dah-mya? Do you have any children?"

"Yes, Thakin. I have a wife and one little girl. But I don't think we will have the little girl very much longer." The chief's dark eyes reflected his sadness. "She's very thin, Thakin, and she's always sick."

"Your little girl is sick!" echoed Harry. "This must be providential. God has arranged this meeting. My friend, who is waiting at the bullock cart, is a white-man doctor. He knows how to cure sick little girls. You go home, Dah-mya, and get your wife and daughter and bring them to our mission station at Shee-hseng. That's where we're going now. Do you know where it is? You do? Then come as soon as you can, for we are staying there only a short time and then the doctor has to return to Rangoon."

They left the chief at the edge of the clearing and prodded the bulls as fast as they could back to the road. Harry knew that Frank would be worried, and wondering about their fate.

"We got them back," he shouted as soon as they came within sound of the trail. "The whole thing was providential, Frank."

Hteelun harnessed the bulls to the cart, and the rest of

the journey to Shee-hseng was uneventful. During their second day at the outstation, the tall bandit chief and his sturdy wife appeared with their little girl. Frank easily diagnosed the child's illness as roundworm infestation, and a dose or two of worm medicine took care of that.

The grateful parents reported back to the station some months later when Harry was there on another visit. The bandit chief's little daughter was growing plump and healthy, and the missionaries had made another circle of friends.

WITCH DOCTOR'S CURE

13 IN THE third decade of the twentieth century, itinerating in the Federated Shan States was not only dangerous but lonely work, and Harry often found he was the only white man for hundreds of square miles. The tribals regarded him with fear or respect, according to the state of their conscience, for in their minds "white man" and "government agent" were synonymous, and who knew what this stranger might be after?

Harry's linguistic ability usually dispelled their suspicions, and as he moved among them, speaking Burmese and quickly picking up a working knowledge of the local dialects, most of them accepted him as a man of Payah-Thakin (God). Harry never missed an opportunity to tell the gospel story and to find out how receptive his listeners were. Would they be willing for a Christian school to open in their village, or a clinic?

Often his long journeys took weeks. By day, Harry hiked hour after slow hour beside the plodding bulls or rode uncomfortably in the creaking cart, trying to read as they swayed along. Sometimes he and his helpers left the cart and pushed their way along jungle trails to remote villages, where the Word of God had never penetrated. At night they cooked their simple meal over a campfire and slept wherever they could find safe shelter.

One night as they made camp seventy or more miles from home, Harry's servant opened the tucker (food) box and reported, "Thakin, we have no dried beans left, and no onions, and only two matches in the box."

Harry's good-natured sigh registered resignation. This boy had been with him for months, and again and again Harry had tried to impress upon him the necessity of reporting to him when goods were getting low so that they could be replaced. He must not wait until the boxes were empty and they were camped in the middle of the deepest jungle, because he, Harry, could not snap his fingers and produce flour or dried beans or kerosene out of thin air. But Hpo-toke, like all his race, was used to living life on a day-by-day basis and could not readily adapt to a thakin's ways.

"All right, Hpo-toke. Fortunately we're only half a mile or so from a village. Go along and find out when the next market is being held in this district, so we can buy those things and maybe even some fruit and fresh vegetables. That'd be a welcome change, wouldn't it?"

Hpo-toke's face was all smiles as he trotted off. Within half an hour he was back with an even wider grin brightening his brown face.

"We are fortunate, Thakin. They hold market every five days and tomorrow is the fifth day, and the marketplace is just over there."

Harry looked to where the boy pointed through the trees to a cleared space on their right that was certainly a market site. An acre or more of brown earth pressed solid under the impact of countless bare feet, with wooden skeletons of leaf-roofed stalls, some with tattered, sun-bleached awnings hanging limp and hoary in the fading light, others older, even more decrepit, leaning at crazy angles against their neighbor for support. A desolate sight, but Harry knew that in the morning the whole area would be throbbing with life and all the sights, sounds, and smells of market day.

Long before sunrise, Harry awakened to the creak of carts and the drone of muffled voices. "Why must they begin so early," he yawned, striking a match to look at his pocket watch. "It's not four o'clock yet."

Yawning again, he reached over the side of his camp cot,

fumbling for his boots, giving each one a hard bang on the ground and a sharp shake before putting it on. Scorpions, spiders, and other tiny creatures shared the nasty habit of hiding inside unworn footwear, as many a white man had found to his sorrow.

Darkness was giving way to dawn when Harry got to the marketplace, but he found that he was too eager. People were still arriving and trading had not begun, so he settled himself at the foot of a young banyan tree and watched the crowd, hoping that soon a peanut vendor would come by with his little charcoal brazier of roasted nuts. His empty stomach rumbled in anticipation of such a treat.

Apart from the opulent few who owned bullock carts, the people came on foot, many of them walking ten to fifteen miles, having started out soon after midnight. Harry watched farmers staggering in, doubled over under the weight of baskets of melons suspended at each end of a bamboo pole carried across their shoulders, their wives trotting alongside, guarding smaller baskets of dubious eggs or scrawny, squawking chickens. Coolies came in, balancing bags of peanuts or upland rice on their heads, and youngsters lugging a pumpkin or a couple of cucumbers.

Regular merchants came too. Worldly-wise fellows who made a living traveling from market to market with their goods. They sold glass bangles and gaudy ribbons, packets of needles and bunches of safety pins, razor-sharp knives, combs and small spotty mirrors, tin funnels and pots and pans, hurricane lamps and hanks of coarse jute string, brightly painted tin toys and many shiny knickknacks guaranteed to entice the ignorant villagers to part with their hard-earned money.

Not that the people had much in the way of cash. Little money changed hands on market days, but brisk bartering of goods went on until all the produce was disposed of, all the necessities obtained, and all the local gossip exchanged. Then the fifth-day merchants packed up their goods and left until next market day.

From the shelter of his tree, Harry watched a farm couple labor up the hill and halt a few yards away. They

carried huge baskets of vegetables at the end of their
shoulder poles, and from their weary, dusty appearance,
Harry judged that they had walked a long distance.

The woman seemed to be in great distress. She dropped
her baskets and tore off her blanketlike headcloth to wrap
around her shivering body. Her sweat-soaked cotton blouse
clung wetly to her ample bosom, and her bright floral longi
afforded little protection against the early morning chill.
For a moment or two she stared blankly around, and then
her sturdy legs crumpled and she sank to the ground,
moaning and rolling back and forth in semidelirium.

Behind her, the man carefully lowered his baskets and
shook out his headcloth. He darted back and forth in inef-
fectual efforts to wrap it around his tossing wife before he
gave up and circled about her, wringing his hands and
begging her to be quiet.

From where he stood, Harry heard the woman's teeth
chattering. Malaria, he nodded to himself. No one knew the
symptoms better than he. She's in the ague stage and her
fever is rising, he thought. He wished he had some quinine,
but the long trip had exhausted his medical supplies and
there was nothing he could do to help.

The woman continued to roll and cry out, and the poor
husband looked more and more agitated. Suddenly he
seemed to make a decision. Shoving the four baskets of
vegetables together, he covered them with a tattered cloth,
then shuffled off into the marketplace, apparently in search
of help.

Weak sunshine crept across the fields and reached the
foot of Harry's tree at the same time that the husband
returned with a gaunt, evil-faced individual whom Harry
immediately recognized as a witch doctor.

The two of them bent over the woman, the witch doctor
trying vainly to rub her forehead with some grisly charm he
carried, and the husband grasping her arms, trying to pull
her upright, urging her to be quiet, and let the witch doctor
do his work. But the woman resisted their efforts, shivering,
and moaning louder and louder, until they gave up. Then
the witch doctor stood straight and tall, making magic signs

in the air and taking down his *shan-lwei-aik* ("bag carried from one shoulder").

Harry had seen these bags before, and he knew pretty well what they contained: bunches of dried herbs and bits of bark, dehydrated eyes and organs of snakes and toads and other small creatures, chips of semiprecious stone, seeds and bones and packets of colored powder, and filthy little bottles of unmentionable liquids corked with tightly wound plugs of straw. He shuddered, wondering which of these horrible concoctions the woman would be forced to swallow.

Reaching into his *aik*, the witch doctor pulled out various bark-wrapped bundles and dingy little cloth bags, shaking them, listening to the rattle of the contents and seeming to weigh up the merits of each. Finally he put them all back into the bag and drew out a piece of buffalo horn about nine inches long and sharply pointed at one end. He tested the point with his forefinger and nodded in a satisfied way. But before beginning his treatment, he told the farmer that there was a devil inside his wife, causing her illness, and he must drive it out or she would not recover. His fee for this service was one kyat.

"One kyat!" the poor husband protested, and Harry whistled quietly through his teeth. That was an exorbitant amount for a poor farmer who scarcely saw money from one harvest to the next. For a few minutes the two men argued back and forth while the woman continued to shiver and roll and mutter. But when the adamant witch doctor picked up his *aik* and made as if to move off, the husband reluctantly felt in his cloth waistband, the poor man's bank, and drew out the money.

It seemed to Harry, still unnoticed under his tree, that the witch doctor looked unduly triumphant as he seized the money and tucked it securely into one of the many amulets adorning his skinny frame. Then he began to prance up and down and shout imprecations at the disease-bearing devil. The noise attracted passers-by, and a sizable crowd quickly gathered around the little arena, watching the scene with awestruck eyes. The presence of the crowd seemed to incite the witch doctor to greater efforts. He straddled the woman and poked her with the sharp end of the buffalo horn, explaining in loud asides to the husband that he must punish the devil until it left the woman's body of its own accord.

Faster and faster the witch doctor prodded. His forehead shone with sweat, and his scrawny muscles bulged as he poked. He shrieked shrill curses on the demon, urging it to leave the woman. Harder and harder he worked. His flailing arms wielded the horn spike up and down with the regularity of a machine.

At first the woman tried to escape, but there was no getting away from the frenzied, wild-eyed creature bending over her, frothing at the mouth from his exertions. Screaming with terror she lay in a trembling heap unable to protect herself.

Harry could see that the sharp horn was inflicting terrible punishment, and he wondered whether he should interfere. What if the devil doctor killed his patient? With a prayer in his heart he took a step forward, but at that precise moment the witch doctor stopped his poking and prancing. With heaving chest and panting breath he leaned over the woman and gasped, "Has he gone? Has he gone?"

"*Thwa-bee. Thwa-bee* ["It's gone. It's gone."]." Almost unconscious and writhing in agony, the woman moaned out her reply, and the watching crowd gave one collective, explosive sigh of satisfaction and nodded to one another. Harry suppressed a shudder and wondered what would have happened if the woman had been unconscious and unable to reply or if she had said No.

With an air of tremendous triumph the witch doctor pushed the piece of horn back into his *shan-lwei-aik*. He gestured disdainfully, almost imperiously, at the gaping crowd and they parted respectfully to make way for him. He walked through the impromptu honor guard, and without a backward glance at the patient or her husband, stalked majestically off into the marketplace.

Now that the show was over, the crowd moved off in twos and threes, excitedly discussing this latest exhibition of the witch doctor's skill. Harry slipped away too. If this was the

Shan method of treating malaria, he hoped he would never have one of his attacks while he was alone in their country.

To his astonishment, a few days later Harry saw the woman and her husband in a distant village. Not only was the woman alive but she looked reasonably well.

TREATING A
WITCH DOCTOR'S WIFE

14 TRACHOMA, WHICH Harry always re-
ferred to as sandyblight because the symptoms closely resembled that eye disease of
the Australian outback, was endemic in
some areas of Burma. One year it was particularly severe.

Every day Harry treated sore eyes. He dispensed eye-
drops, ointment, and free advice to everyone who came to
him. At first he tried to institute regular clinic hours so that
his normal work might continue uninterrupted, but he
might as well have tried to harness the disease-spreading
flies and organize them into orderly bands for annihilation.
People came to his door at all hours, and he had not the
heart to turn them away when he knew that a few bathings
with boric solution and a drop or two of Protargyrol usually
made the difference between healthy eyes and permanent
blindness.

One noon as Harry forked the last grains of rice off his
plate, a loud throat-clearing outside the door announced
that someone waited for him. Harry snapped shut the book
he had been reading while he ate, pushed his chair back,
and went to the door.

A plump, middle-aged Burmese stood on the top step. He
greeted Harry respectfully and introduced himself. "I am a
local witch doctor, Thakin. You don't know me, but I have
heard about you, and I want to ask you something."

"Come and sit down." Harry led the way to the covered

part of the veranda and indicated a chair. He knew that his visitor was no ordinary Shan. The man's speech suggested education, even culture. Harry was curious to know what he was doing in this country district and why he wanted to talk to a missionary. Most witch doctors regarded missionaries as business rivals and avoided them like the plague.

The man made himself comfortable in the cane chair, took out his little lacquer box of betel nut, tobacco, and lime, and rolled a wad of the narcotic "chewing-gum" favored in Eastern countries. Popping it into his mouth he chewed with great gusto, spitting blood-red saliva through the cracks in the bamboo veranda floor. And as he chewed he talked.

"Thakin," he said in the Burmese language, "I have not always lived up here in the Shan States. I was educated in Burma. I studied for the priesthood and I know the Buddhist religion backward and forward."

Harry nodded, privately wondering how Buddhism and witch doctorism could mix, but he said nothing and waited for his visitor to continue.

"The people in this district hold me in great respect and come to me for advice and healing. I am a great man in their eyes, and they will do anything I tell them."

The witch doctor talked on for some time, comparing the Burmese way of life with the Shan, touching on local politics and religion and customs, even branching out into Burmese literature and poetry. Harry waited patiently, he knew this was not what the witch doctor had come for, but it was useless to try to hurry him. When he was ready he would reveal the real reason for his visit.

At last it came. "Thakin," the man leaned forward and almost whispered the words. "Thakin, I've come to you because of this eye sickness. My wife has it so badly that she can't see. She can't do anything but sit on the floor all day and moan with the pain. I have tried all my charms and medicines, but none of them have helped her, and I'm afraid that she will be permanently blind. I knew you were here, but I was afraid to come to you before. I know that you Christians mix your Jesus spirit with all your medicines and that might mesmerize her and harm her."

"Oh, no," Harry assured him. "It will do her good. It is true that we mix Jesus' spirit of love with all our medicines and treatments, but it does the patients good. I've treated half the people in this district for sandyblight, and their eyes are better. The Jesus spirit hasn't harmed them."

"Then will you come to my house and see my wife?" The witch doctor squirted one last mouthful of betel juice down a crack and wrenched his fat body out of Harry's easy chair.

"Yes, of course. I'll come right away." Harry went into the house and collected the few items he needed, and the two men set off along the dirt road.

Harry's medical equipment was as sparse as his knowledge, but in the backward areas of the Federated Shan States, where sickness was rampant and hygiene unknown, his simple treatments and preventive measures earned him a reputation far beyond his skill. Indeed, as Harry found when he first came to the district, any white man—trader, government officer, hunter, or missionary—was expected to be able to do anything from doctoring to house building to slaying a man-eater.

As they neared the outskirts of the village, the plump Burmese witch doctor, leading the way to an ordinary bamboo-and-thatch dwelling, said, "This is my house," then disappeared inside. He could do that because he was barefooted, but Harry, encumbered with the trappings of a different culture, had to stop outside and remove his footwear, because he knew it would be considered most impolite for him to enter a Shan house with his boots on.

Setting his boots neatly beside the doorway, Harry waited in his stockinged feet, but when the witch doctor did not reappear, and there was no sound from inside, he coughed a warning and entered the house.

A fat Burmese woman squatted on the floor of the smoke-blackened room, rocking to and fro and pressing the end of her dingy sash to her eyes. She heard the bamboo floor creaking at Harry's approach and tried to struggle to her feet, groping blindly along the edge of the woven-grass mat, seeming at a loss to know where to go.

"Now, Auntie, don't run away." Harry darted forward

and took her by the arm. "You stay right here. I've come to put some medicine into your eyes and make them better."

"No, no, you'll burn my eyes out," she protested, trying to wriggle from his grasp. Although there was no sign of her husband, he had obviously told her that Harry was coming, and probably he was in the next room peering through the cracks in the woven-leaf wall and listening to all that was going on.

"No, I won't." Harry soothed her in Burmese. "I know how to cure this sandyblight. I've put medicine in the eyes of half the people around here and I haven't burned one. They all got better."

"No, no." The frightened woman waved her arms wildly and tried to push him away. "I'll go blind. You'll burn my eyes out."

"You're blind already, Auntie. I'm going to make your eyes better."

Harry dodged out of her reach and prepared his solution. He decided not to use an eyedropper, because in her panic, the woman might break it, and eyedroppers were hard to come by. Instead, he took a teaspoon out of his bag and used it to drop the cooling lotion into her right eye.

"*Ow! Ow!* It's burning," she shrieked. "It's burning my eye out."

"Nonsense, Auntie." Harry's voice was stern. "Don't tell lies. That medicine will cool and heal your poor eyes. Let me put some in the other eye, and tomorrow I'll come back and treat them again, and your sore eyes will soon be well, and you'll be able to see."

He spoke with quiet authority, trying to calm her. But she still squealed and acted like a spoiled child, grabbing his hands and trying to stop him from reaching her eyes. Despite her antics, Harry succeeded in putting the healing drops into the other eye and stepped back.

"There now. Don't touch your eyes. Don't rub them. Let the medicine do its work, and I'll come again tomorrow."

Harry always prayed for his patients, and that night he prayed most earnestly that his simple treatments would cure the woman's eyes. What a lesson it would be to everyone in the district when they found out that the witch doctor could not cure his own wife but had to appeal to the white missionary for help.

When he returned the next day, Harry found the fat woman sitting in her accustomed place on the mat, aimlessly plucking at the edge of her brightly flowered *aingyee.* She turned toward him as he entered, and he asked, "How are your eyes today, Auntie? Can you see?"

"A little," the witch doctor's wife admitted reluctantly. This time when Harry administered the healing drops, her squawks and swipes at the spoon were only token resistance.

Again the witch doctor did not appear, and Harry wondered what was going on in his mind. Was he realizing the futility of his own charms and medicines? Would he admit that the Jesus Spirit was more powerful than the spirits he worshiped?

After a few more treatments, the woman's eyes were completely healed. The redness and soreness disappeared, and she could see perfectly.

"Now, Auntie, be sure that your eyes don't become reinfected," Harry warned on his last visit. "Don't rub your eyes with your dirty hands, and don't wipe them on anyone else's cloth. Be sure to wash your face and hands well with soap, and keep the flies from settling on your eyes."

"Yes, Thakin. Yes, Thakin." There was no squawking and struggling to escape from the white stranger now. Instead, the fat woman listened carefully to his advice and nodded so vigorously that her double chins wobbled.

"Goodbye, and don't forget to tell your husband that it was not only the medicine but the Jesus Spirit that healed your eyes."

"Yes, Thakin." More nods and wobbles.

At the doorway, Harry stepped into his boots and clambered down the bamboo ladder.

Well, that was certainly an experience to write home about, he mused as he trudged back to his bungalow. "Missionary Treats Witch Doctor's Wife." It ought to make the headlines in the mission reports back home.

THE FATE OF OOHNINE'S WIFE

15 "THAKIN! THAKIN!"

Harry set his razor and shaving brush on the edge of the sink and ran to the door. Swirling morning mists still hid the mountains, and he knew that only something urgent would bring anyone to his house so early.

"What's the matter?" he shouted into the mist. Then he saw old Oohnine's figure emerging and he bounded down the steps to meet him.

"What is it, Oohnine? What's happened?"

The old man half-collapsed at Harry's feet, shoulders heaving, breath coming in great shuddering gasps. Harry grabbed his arms and held him upright; the poor man must have run all the way from Yinmabin. Something terrible must have happened. Anxiously he waited for Oohnine to speak.

"My—wife—Thakin—a tiger—has eaten—her."

Used as he was to hearing tragic announcements, Harry stood for a moment, wordless. Then, in case his old friend was exaggerating and there might still be a chance of saving the woman, he shook Oohnine's arm urgently. "When? How? Tell me quickly, Oohnine."

"Early this morning." Oohnine's leathery old face crinkled into fresh lines of grief. "We found her remains at sunrise—only her head—and bits of her backbone."

Harry's horror mounted. Could it be possible? He'd seen wrinkled old Daw Thane only a few days ago, bent double

under a heavy load of firewood. She was on her way to
Yinmabin, where woodcutters, who supplied the voracious
wood-burning train engine, lived in a huddle of bamboo huts
sprung up in the jungle like mushrooms in the grass.

Harry took the old man's arm and steered him toward
the steps.

"Come upstairs, Uncle. I'll call my servant to heat you
some milk."

Shivering from shock and exhaustion the old hunter had
to be half-pushed up the steps. He sank onto the mat in
Harry's big room and leaned his back against the wall while
he continued his story.

"It was a big tiger. We followed its tracks half a mile
from our village before we found——"

"Yes, yes." Harry tried to divert him from the harrowing
details. "But tell me what happened. Why did the tiger
attack?"

**While the villagers slept, a big tiger entered the hut and
carried off Oohnine's wife.**

"Last night there were about ten of us asleep around the fire in my hut, and a tiger crept in and grabbed Daw-Thane around the waist. She yelled and screamed, and we all woke up. I grabbed a log from the fire and thrust the burning end into his face, and some of the other men beat his rump with their sticks. He didn't want to let go, but there was so much noise and commotion that finally he let her drop, and we drove him out, but he was angry and went away snarling."

Oohnine sipped the hot, sugared milk the servant brought, and his teeth stopped chattering. He pulled the coat Harry had given him more tightly about his shoulders before going on.

"We stayed awake for a long time talking, and asking ourselves, why did the tiger choose Daw-Thane? There were four others sleeping on mats nearer to the doorway than she was, yet it stepped over them and picked her up."

"Was she hurt?"

"Not much, Thakin. The tiger's teeth scratched her body a little, but her clothes protected her. She was terrified, though, and screamed and squawked for a long time before she went to sleep again.

"We stoked the fire up well and took turns watching in case the tiger returned, but toward morning, the one watching feel asleep. You know how it is, Thakin, we had worked hard all day cutting firewood for that big black monster that gobbles up wood faster than I can drink this milk."

Harry nodded. He knew how hard the woodcutters worked. He had often visited their ramshackle bamboo huts, built a few feet above ground, with a clay fireplace in the middle of the floor, and neither doors nor windows to hinder the escape of smoke. What easier place for a hungry tiger to find his dinner?

"No one heard the tiger leap into the hut and once again step over four men to reach Daw-Thane. This time he must have grabbed her around the throat so she couldn't scream when he carried her off.

"When we awoke at sunrise to begin our day's work we discovered that she was gone, and it didn't take long to find out what had happened. There was a blood spot at the doorway and deep pug marks in the dust outside where the tiger had jumped down.

"We shouted and grabbed our knives, and men from the other huts joined us. We all followed the tiger's trail through the village, where the imprints in the dust were plain, and over them a draggy sort of mark made by her skirt or her heels where they touched the ground."

Harry shuddered and opened his mouth, but before he could speak, Oohnine went on:

"Some of the other men found her remains in a thicket, not far from the path we use every day." He paused, his shoulders hunched, and a hopeless look came into his tired eyes as he muttered, "It was fate, Thakin. We could do nothing. Daw-Thane's time had come."

Harry knelt on the floor beside Oohnine and laid a comforting hand on his scarred shoulder as he told the old hunter again about a God of love who understands our sorrows and perplexities.

Often, during their long treks through the jungle, they had talked about God, and many times Harry told the old man one of his own experiences of God's care, particularly of the time when he and sixteen Burmese porters had been forced to spend the night in the open, far up on a lonely mountainside, and in the morning had seen the pug marks which told them that a huge tiger had prowled to within four feet of Harry's camp cot and then retreated.

Now he repeated the story, ending with an earnest plea, "You see, Uncle, God promises in His Book that He will send angels to protect those who trust Him. If only you and Daw-Thane——"

But Oohnine did not seem to understand. He shook his shaggy head and his faded eyes filled with tears as he said, "Your time had not yet come, Thakin Harry; Daw-Thane's had."

HARRY SLAYS A MAN-EATER

16 HARRY WAITED until the ceremonies and ritual mourning connected with the death of Oohnine's wife were over before suggesting that they go out and try to shoot the tiger. Then he went to Oohnine's humble house.

"Old Overcomer," he said, "there are two guns in my house at present. A big heavy one that could easily kill an elephant, and a light rifle. Either of them will kill the tiger if we get a good enough shot."

"All right, Thakin. I will come with you." Since his wife's death, the old man seemed to have lost some of his fierce, fearless spirit, but he brightened at Harry's suggestion, and together they planned their hunting strategy.

"We'll need a goat to use for bait." Harry fished a handful of coins from his pocket. "Do you think you could buy a nice fat one that would bleat loudly and attract the tiger?"

"Any goat will bleat loudly when it is taken away from its companions." Oohnine nodded his wise old head. "But I will search out a fat, young one for you. White would be best, so that we can see it in the dusk."

"A white one, of course. And where should we go? Where would be the best place for us to sit? Do you know any of this tiger's haunts?"

"Yes, Thakin, I know the very thicket he hides in by day, but it would be suicide for us to approach it. But there are some fine big *ingyin* trees on the way to his drinking place. If we went there early in the afternoon and waited, I'm sure we'd see him before dark."

"Should we build a machan in the tree?"

Oohnine shrugged. "As you like. A few short lengths of bamboo to make a platform between the branches would do."

"We need something to rest our guns on." Harry rubbed his upper arms mechanically as if they already ached. "They get so heavy, we couldn't hold them up for hours on end. Could you see to that too, Oohnine, and I'll bring rope, knife, rifles, bullets, and anything else we're likely to need."

In midafternoon the two set out. Oohnine, carrying half a dozen lengths of bamboo over his shoulder and leading a reluctant goat by its long ears; and Harry, carrying both guns, his pockets bulging with bullets, a coil of stout rope slung around his neck, and a sharp hunting knife in a sheath at his belt.

They picked their way carefully along the jungle path, taking care to avoid cracking twigs or rustling dry leaves. They kept their voices to a whisper so as not to attract the man-eater before they were ready. It took half an hour to reach the *ingyin* trees, and then they had to decide which one provided the best view of the route that the tiger was likely to take as he went to drink at the stream.

When that was agreed on, Oohnine climbed the tree, and Harry passed up the lengths of bamboo, peering through the thick curtain of leaves to watch the old hunter ram them into position. They made a rickety, insecure platform, but anything was better than trying to shoot while perching on a branch like a chicken on a roost.

"Now take the guns," Harry whispered, handing them up. Something of the men's anxiety was transmitted to the goat, and the poor creature crouched under the tree, shivering occasionally, rolling its yellow eyes, and bleating forlornly as Harry tied it securely in place.

"Now, then, you bleat good and loud as soon as I'm safely up the tree." Harry slapped the goat's hairy rump and jumped monkeylike for the lowest branch, climbing up and settling himself beside Oohnine on their makeshift machan.

The usual jungle sounds faded with the setting sun.

Birds ceased to sing and sought their roosts. Sun-loving animals found shelter in dens and caves, and the fortissimo of daytime insects muted into the pianissimo of night's winged inhabitants. Even the goat was silent.

"What's wrong with that goat, Oohnine?" Harry glared down at the blur of white huddled at the foot of their tree. "You said it would bleat loudly, and it hasn't made a sound since I climbed up here."

"Maybe it smells the tiger and is scared."

Minutes marched past as the men watched and waited, alert as sentries at their posts. The rosy western sky dimmed to pale lemon, then mauve. Wisps of sunset-tinged cloud floated like colored pennants across the sky.

"Why doesn't the crazy creature bleat? It will soon be too dark to shoot, even if the tiger comes." Harry's patience thinned. "Look Oohnine, here's a long piece of string and my hunting knife. You climb down and cut a tiny slit in the goat's ear and fasten the end of the string to it."

"No, no, Thakin. It's too dangerous. The tiger might get me."

"Of course it won't. I'll be covering you every moment with my gun."

"No, Thakin. It ate my wife——"

"But we won't even see the tiger unless the goat bleats and calls it up," Harry whispered in desperate undertones. "We're sitting here for nothing."

Oohnine made no reply, and Harry whispered urgently, "All right, I'll do it myself."

In a flash he slid down the tree, held the struggling goat's head between his knees and cut a tiny slit in its ear. Tying the string through it he clambered back to the rickety platform, making as much noise and climbing as fast as he could.

"Now," he panted and jerked the string. But there was not a sound from below. "Come on," he hissed down to the trembling animal. "I don't want to hurt you, but you've got to bleat. I won't let the tiger kill you."

Again he jerked the string. The goat moved slightly but made no other sound, and no amount of pulling and jerking called forth a protest from the terrified creature.

"What rotten luck," Harry groaned. It was too dark now to see even the white blur of goat huddled at the foot of the tree, and too dangerous to risk walking back to the village. There was nothing to do but stay all night in the tree. For all they knew, the cunning tiger might be crouched in the bushes watching, licking his chops, and waiting for them to descend.

Too scared to sleep in case they might fall from the tree and unable to converse louder than in whispers in case they attract the man-eater, if he was not already there, tormented by myriads of bloodthirsty mosquitoes, stiff, and toward morning, drenched with dew, and chilled by a mountain wind, the two hunters passed a miserable night. As soon as it was light enough to shoot by, they slid warily and wearily from the tree.

"Could you take the goat and the heavy rifle back to the village, Oohnine, while I go and shoot a deer for you? That will repay you for sitting up all night in the tree with me."

The old hunter's weary eyes brightened. Fresh meat was always a welcome addition to the villager's plain fare, for though the jungle teamed with game that was easily killed with a white man's rifle, it was not so easily brought down with primitive Shan weapons.

"Yes, Thakin, I can take the goat back. The tiger is not likely to be about in daylight."

"Even if it is, you have the big gun, and I've shown you how to use it."

Pulling the goat after him, Oohnine trudged off in the direction of the village.

Harry's rubber-soled boots made no sound as he turned into the thick jungle and started along one of the trails worn by the paws and hoofs of countless animals coming nightly to drink at the stream. Focusing his tired eyes on the trail he tried to sort out the animal tracks. Presently his concentration shattered into a triumphant grin. Clear as print on paper, the fresh hoofprints of a large wild bull overlapped all others.

"What luck! If I can shoot him, it will reward Oohnine

and provide the entire village with beef for a week. I wish I had kept the heavy gun but I guess this one will have to do the trick."

Head down, intent on following the bull's spoor, Harry was startled by a loud snort from the bushes fifty yards ahead. He looked up in time to see the bull toss its head and glare at him before it crashed off through the undergrowth.

"Oh, bother! He's seen me now and knows he's being followed." Harry took extra care to make no sound as he crept forward, following the bull's tracks, raising his head every now and then to scan every foot of the surrounding jungle in the hope of sighting the animal and bringing him down with a long shot.

Once again, the bull snorted from sheltering bushes ahead and dashed off, tail in air, shaking his horns derisively in Harry's direction.

"I'll get you yet." Harry stubbornly plodded on.

A mile farther along the performance was repeated and now it was Harry's turn to snort, "All right, you clever hunk of beef. I'll give you one more chance to show yourself and if I don't get a shot this time I'm going back to the village—if I can find it. I'm starving."

Once more Harry stalked the animal only to hear it snort sardonically and dash for safety when he got within shooting distance.

"All right, you win," he conceded. He felt weak from hunger and loss of sleep, and he had no idea in which direction Oohnine's village lay. He was about to turn back and begin his search when he heard the bull snort again. It had not run far. Looking up quickly, he glimpsed a tawny animal slink into a nearby thicket.

Harry gasped with fright and backed up against the nearest refuge, a clump of half-grown bamboos. In a flash he realized what had happened. While he stalked the bull, the tiger had been stalking him, and now, as it was preparing for its final spring onto its unsuspecting victim, it had seen the bull and the bull had scented the tiger.

Ignoring Harry, the two deadly enemies faced each other for long, nerve-stretching minutes. Then the tiger roared a challenge, and the fight began. Snarling and spitting, the tiger leaped forward, bounding high into the air in its attempt to spring onto the bull's back and with one swift wrench break its opponent's neck. But the bull knew the tiger's tactics. Bellowing with rage, it pounded the earth and tossed its head wildly, trying to pin the tiger with its murderous horns. Both animals knew they were in deadly peril, and the battle would go on until the death of one of them.

Harry realized he was in deadly peril too. The clump of half-grown bamboos afforded no protection. Sooner or later, one of the fear-maddened creatures would bump him and that would be the end.

All kinds of wild plans raced through his mind as he shrank back against his pitiful shelter. Should he run for it? Should he try to hide? Would he be able to run to the nearest tree and climb it?

His fear mounted as the jungle reverberated with bellows and roars and the crash of splintering bushes. Around and around the battle raged. Closer and closer to him, until they were only feet away. Harry raised his gun, but it was impossible to shoot either the leaping, furry fury or the sweat-shined leather hide that dodged, and parried, and pawed up clouds of dust. In a desperate attempt to create a diversion and save his own skin, he pointed the gun skyward and fired one barrel.

The effect was instantaneous. Both animals stopped in their tracks, glaring at each other. Only a few feet away, the tiger stood parallel to Harry, its striped body heaving, and foamy saliva dripping from its panting jaws.

Harry was rigid with fear. If the great cat saw him, it could snuff out his life with one giant paw as easily as he could crush an ant. But the tiger stared straight ahead, not daring to shift its gaze for an instant and give its opponent an advantage.

God help me, Harry silently implored. He turned slightly so that his gun pointed directly at the tiger's chest, and fired the second barrel.

Screeching with pain, the huge cat bounded into the air,

turned in the direction of the sound and sprang straight at Harry. Instinctively, Harry ducked, and the heavy animal curved over his head and crashed into the bamboos behind.

Without waiting to see what happened next, Harry ran as he had never run before, plunging through bushes, scrambling over rocks, tripping on entangling vines. On and on and on, until his trembling legs could take him no farther. The absence of noise behind assured him that he was not being pursued, and he pulled up, and leaned against a pipal tree for support. His breath came in short, agonized gasps; his pounding heart sounded in his ears like jungle drumbeats.

Worse still, he had no idea in which direction he had run. For a long time Harry drooped against the tree, thinking over his terrifying experience; thanking God for saving him. He was hungry, thirsty, tired to the point of exhaustion. But he was alive, and somehow he would find his way home.

Shouldering his gun, he started off again. Oohnine's village lay east of the jungle. He squinted at the sun, his knowledge of the bush surfacing.

It was nearly noon when Harry stumbled onto a well-worn path. The raucous barking of pariah dogs, coming nearer, sounded like sweet music in his ears. He saw the ramshackle huts, with a huddle of women around the village well. Minutes later he collapsed, thankfully, at the foot of Oohnine's bamboo ladder.

The villagers crowded eagerly around him. "What did you shoot, Thakin? Did you get a deer for us?"

Harry shook his head. "I shot the tiger." He brushed a couple of yelping dogs aside and struggled to his feet. "There is a government reward of one hundred kyat on that tiger's head. If some of you will come back with me this afternoon and carry it, you can have the money and I'll keep the skin as a trophy."

The villagers recoiled, muttering and shaking their heads. "Ah no, Thakin, that man-eater is cunning. It's likely you only wounded it, and it will be hiding somewhere waiting to attack us. No, no. We have more regard for our lives than you seem to have for yours."

"You may be right, but my rifle was only inches from its chest when I pulled the trigger. I'm sure it is dead by now." He shrugged. "But I'm not going back unless someone comes with me to help me skin and carry it."

No one offered. Not even Oohnine, who staggered sleepily from his hut to hear the story.

Harry was too tired to care, and after he ate a belated breakfast he walked the long miles back to his own bungalow.

Six days later, a hunting party from Oohnine's village found the dead tiger lying a few yards from the trampled battlefield that Harry had described to them. Its decomposing body had ruined the skin and prevented certain necessary identification, so the government officer refused to give them the reward.

"Ah, well," Harry mused when he learned the end of the story, "at least the man-eater is dead, and Oohnine's wife is avenged."

SEEKING A ROGUE

17 "HAVE YOU heard about the rogue elephant?" the villagers asked Harry. "The government has put a price on his head. One hundred kyat for the man who kills him."

"Yes," Harry nodded. "I've heard about the mad elephant, but I didn't know about the reward."

For months the elephant had terrorized the countryside, and finally the villagers' complaints moved the district officer to offer a reward to anyone who killed the animal and showed its tusks to him.

From the villagers, Harry learned that elephants live as long as human beings, usually about fifty to seventy years and occasionally up to one hundred years. Sometimes an old male elephant became must, mad, and quarrelsome, and the rest of the herd would not have anything to do with him. Then he became a dangerous foe who killed, not for food, as a man-eating tiger or leopard does, but for sheer, wanton destruction.

Back in the second decade of this century, one hundred kyat was a large sum of money, but, much as they coveted it, the villagers had little hope of earning such a fortune. Few of them owned firearms, and bows and arrows and swords were useless for hunting a rogue. They could dig a pit-trap, but that took a lot of time and energy, and very likely they would end up trapping the wrong elephant. Consequently, rewards were usually earned by British Army officers who spent their leave hunting an outlawed animal. Bristling with guns and backed by dozens of bustling beaters who tracked the wanted animal and maneuvered it toward the spot where the thakin waited with his gun, these hunts were wildly exciting events for everyone except the prey. A large portion of the reward money was used to pay the beaters, but the successful hunter rightfully claimed the ivory tusks and the elephant's feet as his.

Stories of the rogue elephant's depredations were uppermost in Harry's mind one afternoon as he prowled through Elephant Jungle. He was curious to see this animal, and when he spied tracks and fresh heaps of dung, indicating that a herd of elephants was ahead of him on the trail, he decided that he must catch up with them and see whether the mad bull was with the herd.

Harry's heart pounded as he pressed furiously after the herd. He knew that he would learn little from seeing their hindquarters. Somehow he must get in front of them and find out whether one had a broken tusk, the chief characteristic of the must bull. As he raced along, Harry made his plans.

Trampled grass and uprooted bamboos indicated that the herd was very conveniently making its way along a track that followed the ridge of the hill. A sandy gully about twenty feet deep ran parallel to the ridge. If he ran along the gully and got ahead of the herd he might be able to cross their path and turn them back to a clear place where he could have a proper look at them.

Putting his thoughts into action, Harry hurried as fast as possible over the unstable sand. The sounds of the elephants feeding guided him, and he kept on going until he was well ahead of them.

The jungle still dripped from the latest monsoon shower, and as he scrambled up the muddy bank and onto the ridge track, Harry knew that his scent would linger in the moist air and be picked up when the herd approached.

He crossed and recrossed the trail several times. He ran his hands over his sweaty face and wiped them down the smooth bark of a nearby tree. He did everything he could to ensure that there would be plenty of human scent for the leading elephant to identify.

For a few moments Harry stood and listened to the crack of bamboos that accompanied the elephants' progress, then he leapt down the bank and ran back along the gully. He needed to hurry if he wanted to reach the spot he had in mind before the elephants panicked.

Harry kept running back over the sand until he rejoined the jungle track near the place where he first noticed the elephant spoor. A short way from there, the track ran through a small glade ringed with teak trees whose huge leaves afforded splendid cover. Just the right place, Harry decided as he selected a tree on the opposite side of the glade and hid behind the stout trunk.

During the wet season he covered his topee with a protective green oilskin, and he knew that when he peered around to watch the approaching elephants his head would be indistinguishable from the large green leaves above him. Elephants have poor eyesight and depend mainly on their sense of smell to locate enemies. So long as the wind continued to blow toward him, carrying his scent away from them, he would be safe.

Harry had his trusty "spirit of death" gun with him, and although he had no intention of using it except in an emergency, he grasped it tightly to his side, gaining courage from the feel of cold steel. He waited, listening, his suspense mounting when he estimated that the elephants must be nearing the crest of the hill. Would they get his scent and turn back as he hoped? His heart nearly stopped beating when he heard an elephant's distant squeal. The lead cow had caught his scent.

Wild elephants have an inborn dread of man, and at the cow's frenzied trumpetings, the terrified herd turned and stampeded back down the trail. Harry felt the ground shuddering under their pounding feet and heard the bushes and trees splintering as their heavy bodies crashed through the undergrowth. The cows kept up a shrill, excited trumpeting, and Harry began to have misgivings about his clever idea. What if the herd kept on coming at this pace and in this mood? Would he be able to climb his teak tree quickly enough to get out of their way? Would the tree be strong enough to withstand the force of their attack if they saw or smelled him?

Fortunately, by the time they reached the far side of the glade their alarm had worn off, and they ventured out, one by one, waving their trunks wildly back and forth, snuffing the air, and lining up until there were twelve of them standing abreast, staring across the glade, bodies swaying, and forelegs restlessly thumping the ground.

Harry kept perfectly still, scarcely daring to blink or breathe. The animals remained lined up, side by side, like cattle about to be judged at an agricultural show. The elephants were aware of Harry's presence, but their irresolution gave him plenty of time to examine them. Beginning with the lead cow, he scrutinized each one carefully, looking for a broken tusk. They were all whole. The old rogue was not among them.

The old rogue was not among them, but in the center of the lineup of cows and bulls, one massive animal held Harry's fascinated gaze. A huge bull with long, thick tusks that instead of being parallel, crossed each other about midway along their length. When the animal wanted to raise his trunk he had to maneuver it around and lift it up inside the space of the crossed tusks. Feeding must have presented a real problem, but the animal looked as fat and healthy as the others, and Harry could only wonder how and why the deformity had arisen.

He would have given a fortune (if he had one) for a camera to record that picture. As far as he knew, he was gazing at the only cross-tusked elephant in all of Burma, perhaps the only one in the world, but no one would believe his story without evidence. He had not heard any of his Burmese friends talk of seeing this animal, and yet it must have roamed the jungle for many years.

Harry would have been content to watch the elephant lineup for the rest of the day, but the animals apparently had better things to do than stand staring at a circle of teak trees, so presently the end one snorted disdainfully, as if to say, What idiots we are, standing here like this. Let's get going. And with another disgusted snort he turned and led the way back into the jungle.

Harry watched the herd disappear, following their progress up the ridge by the sound of their thunderous belly rumblings and then by the distant cracking bamboos and occasional indignant squeals when two cows grabbed for the same bunch of leaves. Gradually even these sounds grew fainter, and he was preparing to leave when, *swish-swash*, a closer noise suddenly startled him and he swung around to find an old cow elephant standing right behind him.

Petrified, he waited for her curling trunk to wrap itself around his body and dash him to the ground, so her huge feet could mash him into pulp. But the trunk waved aimlessly above his head, swish-swashing around, investigating the leaves and branches of the teak tree. Gradually Harry's racing heartbeats returned to normal, as he realized that the poor old creature was blind. Keeping perfectly still, he looked up into her eyes, which were white-filmed and glazed. She was so thin that her crinkled skin hung in pleats and folds on her bony frame. Her sense of smell must have deteriorated too, for she did not notice Harry's presence at all and carefully edged her way around the tree that protected him, guided by her searching trunk until she cleared the obstruction and plodded slowly up the track. Perhaps she followed the herd by instinct only, for it seemed that age had impaired all her vital senses.

Harry breathed a sigh of relief and stood watching until she was out of sight. Then, picking up his trusty gun, he thankfully made his way back home. He had had enough excitement for one afternoon.

TWENTY GOATS FOR DINNER

18 EVEN HARRY'S bachelor eyes could see that the Burmese teacher's baby was not doing well. It cried a lot—a low, insistent wail with a note of hopelessness about it, and it lay back in its mother's arms, listless and pale, its exposed hands and face the color of old ivory, so different from the olive-skinned, rosy-cheeked school-children running and shouting nearby.

"Maung-Hpo-Yin, what is wrong with the baby?" Harry came into the schoolroom where the young Burmese teacher sat preparing a lesson for the afternoon session. "Why does it cry so much?"

The young teacher's face remained expressionless but he spread his hands in a despairing gesture. "My wife has not enough milk for him."

"Ah!" Harry nodded. He knew that numbers of Asian babies died before they were a year old, not only from disease, but often because their mothers did not know how to feed them during the weaning process.

Harry was not the person to stand by and see anyone suffer, not if he could do something about it. At the first opportunity he yoked his precious bulls to the creaking old bullock cart and trekked thirty miles to the goat market.

Fortunately for him trade was slack that day, and he purchased a whole herd of goats—nineteen nannies and one old grandpa of a billy with a beard draggling down to the ground, and an odor that carried for a mile when the wind was right, and loaded them into his cart.

"Now Maung-Hpo-Yin," he announced to the surprised teacher, as the bleating cartload trundled into the schoolyard, "here is a whole herd of goats for you. Now there will always be milk for your little baby. Get the schoolchildren to help carry branches and bamboos, and there is some old timber behind the mission house. We must build a strong pen for these goats."

The teacher's impassive face broke into a smile, and he jumped up and called to the bigger schoolboys and girls. Together the whole excited group accompanied Harry and the cartload of goats through the schoolyard and into the teacher's backyard.

It took hours of hard work. The men dug deep holes for the corner posts, while the older boys and girls ran to the nearest part of the jungle and cut down bamboo. The younger children scurried back and forth fetching nails, hammer, and string from the mission house.

"We must make it very strong, Thakin," Maung-Hpo-Yin observed, holding an end of rope between his strong, white teeth, "or the leopards will get the goats. Every night they come sniffing around in the town. Last week they nearly got my dog."

"Why don't you take the dog into your house at night?" Harry knew that next to his wife and little son, the skinny fox terrier was the pride and joy of Maung-Hpo-Yin's heart. Every town and village had its curse of pariahs, mangy mongrels that thieved, scratched, and fought in the streets, but not many families could afford the luxury of a pet dog, one that was fed and taught to do tricks, as Maung-Hpo-Yin's dog was.

"It is too hot, Thakin. He prefers to sleep on the veranda, but I have fixed things so that the leopards won't get him. See," he pointed across the diminishing pile of building materials to the door of his house where a neat little fox-terrier-sized hole cut into the bottom provided a way of escape for the animal. "When he smells the leopard he comes inside."

"Good idea."

Harry thought his goat pen would be leopard-proof, but the determined animal ripped a hole through the roof.

It was nearly sundown when Harry hammered in the last nail and stood back to admire the goat pen. It looked substantial enough to withstand a herd of elephants, but he circled it carefully, kicking the walls with all his might, shouldering the door and pushing with all his strength. "I think it will do," he panted to Maung-Hpo-Yin. "I hope you made the roof good and strong."

With due ceremony the goats were driven into their leopard-proof enclosure each evening, and with equal ceremony Maung-Hpo-Yin's wife milked the four lactating nannies each morning and set the whole herd loose to graze all day in the surrounding fields. For a few days all went well. The goats adapted to their new home, the baby adapted to goat's milk, and Harry congratulated himself on his farsightedness.

But one night a particularly hungry leopard smelled goat and fancied a meal of goat meat. While everyone slept he prowled round and round the enclosure, growling and snarling and trying to stampede the frightened goats into breaking loose. But Harry's pen was strong. The leopard could not get in, and the goats could not get out. In a fury of frustration the determined animal leaped onto the roof and clawed a hole large enough to let him drop inside.

The terrifying uproar awakened Maung-Hpo-Yin and his wife, and they listened, trembling and helpless, while the persistent beast killed a goat and climbed outside with its burden.

In the morning only a few cracked bones, smears of blood, and some raggy scraps of goat hair showed where the leopard had dined.

"Well, that's the end." Harry's voice was dull with disappointment. "It's no use replacing the roof and trying to keep him out. Nothing will stop a determined leopard. I've heard the most incredible tales of what they can do."

Maung-Hpo-Yin nodded, and Harry, interpreting the despondent expression on his brown face, hastened to cheer him. "Don't worry about the baby, Maung-Hpo-Yin. I'll send to Rangoon for some baby formula. It can come up with the next lot of school supplies."

Harry was correct about the leopard. Once it had the taste of easy meat it came night after night and carried off a goat until only the old billy was left. Apparently his body odor was too much for even a hungry leopard to stomach.

"What'll we do with him?" Harry and Maung-Hpo-Yin stood outside the now empty goat pen watching old billy sauntering majestically from one tuft of grass to the next, nibbling only the tenderest shoots with the air of a connoisseur.

"The townspeople are having a feast on Friday. They might like to buy him."

"He'd make pretty tough eating."

"They eat worse things than that—snake, dog, and turtle. I'll take him down when school is out this afternoon."

As soon as old billy was disposed of, and the fine strong goat pen put into use as a school storeroom, Harry considered the entire episode closed, but he reckoned without the leopard.

Every night or two it came back to the mission station, prowling through the schoolyard and around the teacher's house, climbing up onto his veranda in vain efforts to catch the little fox terrier unawares. The hunt became a war of nerves in which the humans came off second best.

"We don't get any sleep, Thakin," Maung-Hpo-Yin complained. "The leopard comes around, and the little dog bolts inside and cowers close to us, shaking and shivering with his hair standing on end like a brush; and the leopard paces up and down the veranda, sniffing at the hole in the door, snarling, pushing his paw through, and clawing at anything he can reach. My wife is terrified that he will break down the door and eat us."

"I don't think that's likely, but I'll lend you my gun." Harry walked to his house and fetched a light rifle and some bullets. "This gun is loaded, Maung-Hpo-Yin, so be very careful how you handle it. This is the safety catch. First you push that off—like this. Then you point the muzzle at the leopard and pull the trigger. Afterwards you have to reload the rifle. Now watch, and I'll go through it all again."

Maung-Hpo-Yin took the rifle as happily as if it had been red hot. He had never held one before, and though he listened carefully to all the instructions, Harry doubted whether the teacher knew the barrel from the butt.

Oh, well, I don't suppose he can do much damage. He's not likely to aim at anything inside his house, and there won't be anything outside except the leopard, and that's what he's supposed to shoot at. Harry shrugged and went back to his work at the mission.

Soon after dark that very night, Harry heard a single shot ring out. He grinned to himself and wondered whether the teacher had shot the leopard.

Morning light revealed no dead leopard, and no blood marks that would signify a wounded one. But it did bring loud lamentations from a farmer living farther down the hill when he discovered that his horse had been killed and half of it eaten by a very hungry and a very-much-alive leopard.

THE DOCTOR'S DOG

19 "ONLY FIVE thousand inhabitants!" The doctor's eyebrows shot up. "There must be as many wild animals around here as there are people."

Harry nodded. "Taunggyi has been my headquarters for years, and it's a paradise for hunters. No matter how much game they shoot, there's always more."

"Have you done much shooting?" The doctor was new to the district and eager to learn.

"Not much. I killed a man-eater once, and I usually carry a gun for self-defense, but I don't like to shoot God's creatures unless it is necessary."

The doctor leaned over the rail of Harry's house, his keen eyes roving from mountain top to valley. Outside the perimeter of Taunggyi, jungle trees and undergrowth covered the area as thickly as the hairs on a tiger's skin, and marred only by village clearings as ugly as battle scars on an otherwise perfect hide.

"Leopards are the biggest nuisance." Harry flicked a fly off the back of his hand. "They're almost a plague in this district. Every evening they come into the town and prowl the streets in search of dogs. They love dog meat, and there's scarcely an animal left here that hasn't had a narrow escape."

A wry smile flickered across the doctor's face. "From the little I've seen of village life, there always seem to be dogs enough and to spare."

Harry laughed. "Oh, you mean the pi-dogs, the pariahs that nobody owns. Leopards eat them too, but they've lived by their wits since they were pups, and they're so cunning that as soon as the sun sets, they slink into the nearest house and hide. Don't be surprised anytime to find a pi-dog under your bed."

"I'll close the doors at six o'clock." The doctor chuckled and then grew more serious as he fondled the ears of the beautiful creature at his side. "I'll have to watch mine. She's a pedigreed bitch and very intelligent. My wife would be heartbroken if anything happened to Rani."

The men talked for a while longer, the conversation drifting from the nearby army camp, and the government headquarters' buildings, to the mission schools, and other Adventist work in the district.

"It takes a long while to break through," Harry explained. "Most of the hill people are animists and extremely fatalistic in their attitude. Buddhism is strong among the Burmese in big towns and cities. I've had many interesting talks with the pongyis once I have earned their confidence, and for that one needs to know the language, customs, and beliefs pretty well. You know, doctor, a couple of times I've sat all night in a monastery talking, discussing their religion, and ours. They have legends passed down through countless generations that are amazingly similar to the Bible account of the Creation and the Flood in Noah's day."

"But they don't believe in any God, do they?"

"No, they say the world always was and always will be a place of sin, sickness, and sorrow. Their aim is to divorce themselves entirely from their worldly desires that, they say, only bring ultimate unhappiness, and to try to attain enlightenment by meditation and good works. It is hard for a Westerner to follow their reasoning."

The doctor picked up his topee and snapped his fingers at Rani. "Well, I'd better go and finish settling in. I can see we're going to have a busy time up here."

It was not many weeks after the doctor's visit that someone reported that the doctor's beautiful pet had been killed and eaten by a leopard.

"That's the limit!" Harry exclaimed, remembering what the doctor had said about his wife's attachment to Rani. "We'll have to do something to try and get rid of these pests. Maung-Htoon-Mya, where are you?"

There was no answer and Harry went to the door and called downstairs: "Maung-Htoon-Mya ["Mr. Bright Emerald"], come here."

"Yes, Thakin." The servant boy came running.

"Maung-Htoon-Mya, there's a length of rope out in the shed. I want you to go to the bazaar and catch one of those stray dogs that skulk around there and bring it back to me."

Maung-Htoon-Mya's face was one big question mark. "What do you want it for, Thakin? Those dogs are no good, they're all mangy and skinny. The doctor wouldn't like one of those dogs."

Harry hid a grin and waved him off. "I'll tell you when you come back. Hurry and find one."

Spurred on by his native curiosity Maung-Htoon-Mya found a length of rope and ran off to the bazaar. In a short time he was back, dragging a skinny, protesting pi-dog in his wake.

"Now Maung-Htoon-Mya, we're going hunting, and this wretched animal will be our lure. Give it some food and water, and hurry through your work. We'll leave about five o'clock, or as soon as I finish off these mission books."

Even in the pleasant climate of Taunggyi, five thousand feet above sea level, mountain climbing was hot, hard work. By the time Harry and Maung-Htoon-Mya had covered another two thousand feet to the stream that Harry had in mind, they were glad to sit and rest, and watch the sun sink behind the massive trees that overlooked a narrow path. Many paths led to a drinking place scored by the multitudinous tracks of jungle creatures. Harry tied the dog to a stout branch opposite the tree that he himself planned to sit in.

He beckoned to his servant boy. "Come on, Maung-Htoon-Mya, we'll sit up here. When a leopard comes to drink and smells this dog—which shouldn't be hard—I'll shoot the leopard. That might scare all the leopards away from town for a while."

The two climbed into the tree, and Harry cleared a space through the leaves so that he could see the dog. He checked his gun and rested it on a branch and pointed it forward. Then he sat back, every sense alert, and waited.

Night flung a cloak of darkness over the mountain, and jungle silence closed in around them. Occasional low patterings, subdued murmurings, munchings, and mumblings of unseen small creatures kept Harry's nerves taut.

While he and Maung-Htoon-Mya waited for the moon to rise, the dog cringed on the ground frozen with terror. Strong leopard smell permeated the drinking place and the dog instinctively knew it must not make the slightest sound that would betray its presence to the enemy.

Just my luck, Harry groaned inwardly as the moon rose, and he saw the animal's fear. Why won't it yelp and yap like all the other village dogs? I won't let the leopard kill it. But I suppose it doesn't know that. Oh, what to do? I suppose the whole business will simply be a waste of time. I wish I hadn't bothered.

Harry's self-recriminations were interrupted by a sharp jab in the ribs. "Leopard has come," Maung-Htoon-Mya whispered.

Harry peered through the leaves in the direction the boy pointed. Pale moonlight flooded the scene and outlined the spotted hide of a leopard crouched on one of the animal trails, its head turned toward the dog.

Without making a sound Harry poked his rifle through the gap in the leaves and aimed it at the leopard's head.

At about the same instant that his finger tightened on the trigger, the mangy dog gave a terrified yelp. With a desperate tug it broke the tethering rope and tore off into the jungle. The leopard bounded after it.

Harry groaned as both animals disappeared, and sounds of the chase died away. Well, that's that. Another good idea gone west.

Now it was too dangerous to climb down and attempt the walk back to Taunggyi. Who knew how many more leopards lurked beneath the trees—or tigers, or wild boars, or deadly snakes? It didn't take much thinking for Harry to decide that they must stay where they were until morning. With a resigned sigh he tied his gun to a branch and settled back as comfortably as he could. Maung-Htoon-Mya was higher up in the tree, and Harry heard him rustling around in search of a better perch.

"Careful you don't go to sleep and fall down," he warned. "Leopards are not the only animals around here."

A grunt was his only reply. Clearly his servant took a dim view of the entire proceedings.

With his lure gone, there was no need for Harry to remain alert. He anchored himself as best he could by hooking his arms and legs around branches and fell into an uneasy, mosquito-haunted doze.

Much later he was prodded back to consciousness by Maung-Htoon-Mya's toe in his ribs. "Thakin. Thakin. I hear a leopard climbing in the tree next to ours." The boy's shaky voice was so low that Harry hardly made out the words. "When it gets as high as we are, it will leap across to our tree and eat us."

Harry knew that the boy's fears were not groundless. Leopards are agile and can climb like cats. He listened intently. Maung-Htoon-Mya was right; there was no doubt that some large animal was climbing the tree a few feet from theirs. As quietly as possible he leaned down, untied his gun and pointed it skyward at an angle away from both Maung-Htoon-Mya and the unknown animal, and fired.

A shower of leaves and twigs rained down, followed by frantic scufflings and slidings in the neighboring tree, and then the thump of a heavy body hitting the ground.

"That's frightened him off," Harry chuckled. "Wonder if it was the same leopard that chased the dog?"

Maung-Htoon-Mya had no ideas on the subject, and Harry went back to his dozing. Finally the long night ended, and he was able to climb stiffly from the tree. Maung-Htoon-Mya followed him down, yawning and rubbing his eyes.

Harry yawned too. "Come on, let's get home for breakfast and our day's work."

HIKE TO LOI-LIM MOUNTAIN

20 IT SEEMED incongruous that after working for years in primitive parts of Burma and the Shan States, escaping death and major injury from fang, claw, and sword, Harry fell prey to the tiny, female Anopheles mosquito.

More deadly than man-eaters, these blood-sucking pests operated mainly in the hours before dawn and after dusk. They drew disease-ladened blood from malaria sufferers and passed it on to their next victim, and in many tropical countries there was scarcely a person who escaped the dread ague and fever.

For ten years Harry battled on, plagued by recurring bouts of malaria and blackwater fever, until finally the sad day came when his ill-health forced him to say farewell to his friends in Taunggyi and the surrounding hills, and go down to live in Rangoon, where he would be near medical help.

He found lodgings in a boarding house close to the big general hospital, so that he could be admitted quickly when he felt an attack coming on. All too frequently he was a patient in the hospital, but in between times he worked as translator for the mission.

Harry was in his element in Rangoon. He loved Burma, and the Burmese was the foreign language he knew best. He worked hard and translated several large books, as well as countless papers and tracts.

The Seventh-day Adventists did not own a printing press in Burma, but Harry was friendly with some of the workers and officials at the big American Baptist Mission printing press, and they undertook to print and bind the books.

The British and Foreign Bible Society also gave Harry a lot of translating work to do, but he still longed for active mission service.

In between his bouts of malaria, Harry felt ready to tackle anything, and often, during school vacations in the summer, the union committee arranged for him to take groups of students on "missionary journeys." These groups went from village to village with Harry, visiting the people in their homes, talking to them about Jesus, and offering simple remedies for their numerous ailments.

Usually Harry was assigned half a dozen of the most promising young men from various schools, but during one vacation he had twelve students working with him. "My disciples," he called them. Most of the boys came from Meiktila Technical School in Upper Burma. They all spoke Burmese, though one was a Chin boy, and two or three were Karens from Eric Hare's district.

They were an eager group, keen to learn all they could, and Harry was equally keen to teach them and give them as much experience as possible. These were the kind of youth that he hoped would later become the backbone of the Adventist work in Burma.

After breakfast one morning, Harry called his "disciples" out onto the veranda of the house where they were staying.

"Do you see that village away up on Loi-lim mountain?"

The group shaded their eyes with their hands and looked in the direction that he pointed. The drifting clouds revealed a huddle of huts and houses clinging precariously to the windswept mountain.

"I've never been to that place, and I've often wondered what kind of people live way up there. What kind of food can they grow on that bare mountaintop? Where do they get water? What religion do they practice? How would you like to come with me, and we'll find out?"

"Yes, yes, Saya-gyi*."

"Yes. Sure."

The "disciples" all agreed with Harry's suggestion, and a babble of excited questions broke out as they crowded around and rapidly made their plans. While the boys collected the few personal supplies they needed, Harry hurried into the house and sorted out a quantity of medicines to take with them, and some bags of rice and lentils. He filled his pockets with tracts, though he doubted that anyone in that mountain settlement would know how to read. Most large villages had a *pongyi-kyaung,* a combined monastery and school where the Buddhist monks, or *pongyis,* taught the children religion and the rudiments of reading and writing. But it was hardly likely that such an isolated place as that mountaintop village would have more than a whitewashed pagoda where the people could worship. In fact, it was probable that they were animists, and not Buddhists at all.

As soon as the group, and all the bundles and packages, were assembled on the veranda, the goods were divided into man-sized loads, and equally distributed, and the "disciples" set off in great good humor—talking, laughing, and singing as they strung out along the narrow trail. Harry led the procession, and one of the older boys walked at the rear. Most of the group wore native dress and went barefooted. A few, like Harry, wore shirts and short trousers, and the long socks and rubber-soled boots favored by Europeans living in hot climes.

Up, up, up they climbed, hour after hour. The laughing died away, and there was less and less breath available for talking and singing. The headloads, light at first, grew heavier with each toiling step. Sweat oozed from brown brows and white, and the group was glad to halt at every turn of the trail, to rest and gulp great draughts of cool water from the trickling streams.

"Not much farther, boys," Harry shouted encouragingly, and pointed up to the last bend of the rocky track. Though he was twenty years older than some of the boys trotting

---

* "Teacher-big." The adjective always comes after the noun in Burmese.

behind him, years of pioneering had toughened his muscles and strengthened his legs so that he easily kept in the lead.

Reaching the top, the group stopped for a last rest and looked back on the fleecy white clouds massed below them like freshly fluffed cotton. "See how high up we are," one of the plainsboys remarked, sounding scared, and his companions teased, "This might be the nearest you'll ever get to heaven, Maung-Ngway-Zin ["Mr. Pure Silver"]. Come along now." And they hustled him on.

The sun had retreated from the valleys and was lingering briefly on the highest hills when the tired group straggled toward the village. Looking around him, Harry found the answers to some of his questions. Hardy vegetables and tiny plots of upland rice grew in small terraced areas wrested from the stony terrain. A few spindly-legged goats wandered among the craggy rocks, nibbling, it seemed, at the bare ground. A spring of icy water on the mountain crest supplied the villagers' needs.

Yapping pi-dogs, erupting from huts and houses, announced the group's arrival, and a startled headman hurried out to greet the visitors. People came running from all directions, crowding around the group, chattering among themselves and staring in amazement at Harry. They had never seen a white man before and excitedly they discussed the phenomenon.

"Do you think his skin really is that color or has he put something on it?"

"Look at his eyes, the color of the sky on a fine day."

"See his hair! It has bends in it like a mountain trail."

"Is he white all over, or only the parts that show? Perhaps he is only white in patches?"

Harry listened, amused at their comments and their childlike curiosity. "No, not just in patches," he assured them. "I'm white all over."

He spoke in a dialect that they understood, expecting them to be surprised that a white man spoke their language, but he was disappointed. It was apparent that as far as these primitive people were concerned, there was no language other than theirs in the whole of Burma. Few of them traveled more than a mile or two from their mountain, and they knew little of the outside world.

Despite Harry's assurances, they still crowded around, giggling and chattering, the more daring ones surreptitiously rubbing his arms or legs to see if the white came off.

Most of the children hung back, wide-eyed and scared, but Harry overheard one tousle-haired girl of about 8 years old, whisper to her mother, "It would never do to tell lies to a white man. He would know immediately. You couldn't deceive him."

"Why?" asked her mother.

Shuddering, the child replied, "Because he has more eyes than a *pin-koo-net.*"

Harry knew that a *pin-koo-net* is an ugly black trapdoor spider, deadly as a snake, causing death if an unwary victim steps barefoot on its hole. But he was at a loss to understand the comparison until he followed the little girl's fascinated gaze and found that she was staring at the fancy pattern woven into the turnover tops of his knee socks. She had never seen any kind of Western clothes before and the pattern must have looked like eyes to her.

"Come inside, Thakin, come." The headman led the way into his house. Harry, his group, and as many of the villagers as could squeeze inside, followed. The rest crowded around the doorway, eager not to miss seeing or hearing anything their unexpected visitors might do or say.

The house was the usual type of Burmese dwelling, with stout wooden corner posts, woven matting walls, and a thatched gable roof. The one big room had a central, packed-clay fireplace for cooking and warmth. In the corners of the roof, the smoke-blackened rafters were festooned with sooty cobwebs, but a lot of the family's possessions hung or were stacked on the middle rafters: a spinning wheel, a crossbow, a wooden plow.

Strings of onions and bunches of dried-leaf spices shared one end wall with two shiny brass ladles, and a huddle of clay cooking pots leaned against the large stone grinding mill.

There was no furniture whatever. Everyone squatted on

the wooden floor, arms clasped around knees, listening intently to everything that was said.

Darkness settled over the mountain and Harry and his "disciples" shivered in the chill wind that whistled through the chinks in the woven walls. They wished they had worn warmer clothing, and Harry marveled that the villagers, who wore little by way of adequate clothing, seemed not to feel the cold.

Presently, the headman's wife began to prepare the evening meal. Harry and his boys brought out their food and added it to their hosts' meager stores, but still it was a poor meal and the chilled, still-hungry Christian group wondered if this was how the village people always felt.

During his conversation with the headman, Harry found that the people were animists, who believed that a god dwelt in every stone and stream and living thing. They spent their whole life trying to appease this spirit and that spirit. The concept of a God who loved them and wanted them to be healthy and happy was entirely new.

Far into the night the villagers packed the big room listening to Harry tell them about Jesus.

Finally, the talking tapered off and the people drifted away to their houses, taking the "disciples" with them. As befitted his position as leader, Harry was invited to remain in the headman's house. Sleeping mats were laid out around the fire, and the headman and his family drew their thin, handwoven blankets over them and settled down to sleep.

Harry lay awake watching the firelight flicker on the rafters. He was no stranger to sleeping on mats on wooden floors, or even to smoky fires, but the split bamboo provided for his pillow threatened to cut off his ear every time he turned his head. He felt cold, too, and huddled up in his blanket trying to stop his teeth from chattering, while he silently berated himself for not having had sense enough to bring more blankets.

Heavy breathing from different parts of the room soon proclaimed that the headman and his family, who seemed immune to discomfort and privation, were asleep.

But Harry could not sleep. He listened to the wind

whistling through the cracks and moaning its way between the houses. A loose bunch of thatch *thwacked* dismally against the rafters, and faint and far-off an animal howled.

"Ouch!" Harry turned his head and grunted with pain as a sliver of split bamboo pierced his neck. Now that they were all asleep he could discard this wretched pillow. He pushed it quietly aside, holding his breath, lest the faint scraping sound disturb his sleeping host, and he be insulted.

He stopped pushing the bamboo piece, but the sound continued. Puzzled, Harry lay quite still, listening. The scraping grew louder and resolved itself into a scratching rustle overhead. Someone, or something, had climbed up and was creeping across the thatched roof.

"Ain-mo-baw-hma-bah-shee-bah-th-doan?" Harry whispered, leaning toward the headman's silent form.

When the old man did not stir, Harry prodded him and repeated urgently, "Headman, what is on the roof of your house?"

"Eh?" The old man raised his head and listened. "It must be a leopard, Thakin. My wife has a few fowls that she keeps under the house with the dogs and goats. But sometimes they roost up on the roof. The leopard must be after them. Don't worry, it can't get inside." He turned over and went to sleep again.

Can't get in? Harry thought of the leopard that had torn the roof off his beautifully constructed goat pen and carried off the goats. He felt positive that this roof was not as secure as the one he and Maung-Hpo-Yin had made. His heart thumped loudly and he lay back listening intently, but the rustling ceased and presently he heard a muffled thud on the far side of the house. Apparently the animal's keen ears had caught their whispered conversation and it had decided to seek its supper elsewhere.

The rest of the night passed reasonably quietly for Harry. The next day, he and his "disciples" went back to Rangoon, hopeful that they had sown some gospel seed in the hearts of the people in the village high up on the Loi-lim mountain.

THE MAD EVANGELIST

21

"THAKIN! THAKIN, wake up. Don't make a noise."

Harry stirred and opened his eyes. A tall, thin Burman bent over him, shaking him by the shoulder. Above the man's head he could see stars shining, brilliant as diamonds on black velvet. Dazed with sleep, Harry blinked and wondered where the ceiling had gone. He sat up and looked around at the huddled mounds of bedclothes lying around him in the open field, and then he remembered.

It all began the day Oo-Pain-Shey—Old Tall and Thin, Harry called him, because he was so thin and so tall—strode into the Rangoon mission office and demanded to see the president. The man was tall and imposing, but there was a wildness in his manner and a strange gleam in his eyes that showed that his mind was unbalanced.

"Ah, Thakin," he said to the president, "I'm a Pwo-Karen man. Up in my area there are thousands and thousands of Pwo-Karens who speak Burmese and are interested in Christianity. You Seventh-day Adventists must come to my area and preach. I'm a man of authority and I have great influence there. You can stay in any village, and I will send word and gather the people from far and near to come and hear you. You will have many converts."

"Yes, yes. Thank you very much." The president smiled and spoke kindly to his visitor and managed to send him off without making any particular promises. The tall Pwo-

Karen was obviously mad, and who wanted to make promises to a madman?

But next day Old Tall and Thin was back again. "Come to my area," he urged. "I'll get you lots of converts. Lots and lots." His eyes glowed and he seemed about to work himself up into a fever of excitement until the president said hastily, "All right. We'll talk it over. Come back next week."

But the garrulous madman did not wait until next week. The next day he was back at the office again. Fortunately, the president was out.

Day after day the wild-eyed Pwo-Karen appeared at the mission office, repeating his story and urging the Adventists to come to his village. Finally, the president called his committee of overseas ministers together.

"What shall we do?" he asked. "This man is obviously unbalanced, but it seems that the only way to satisfy him is to promise to go and preach in his area. Probably he is very well-known and will be able to draw a crowd. He says that all his people understand Burmese."

"But none of us can speak Burmese well enough to preach a whole evangelistic series in it," the secretary objected.

"Harry can. He speaks Burmese like a native."

"But he's been so sick lately. He might not feel up to conducting an evangelistic campaign."

"That's right. I suggest we go for only ten days and let us do the preaching—we can take turns—and Harry can interpret for us."

And that was how it came about that three of the Rangoon ministers and Harry were in the Pwo-Karen district conducting a series of evangelistic meetings. They made Oo-Pain-Shey's village their headquarters, but the rice fields had been harvested and the weather was delightfully mild, so they chose to sleep in the open rather than in the crowded house of their host. The monsoon was long past, and they had no fear of a sudden rainstorm.

"Follow me. I want to show you something." Oo-Pain-Shey's insistent whispering brought Harry back to the present. "Be quiet. Don't awaken the others."

Harry sighed and rolled out of his bedclothes. Squinting up at the stars he judged it to be about midnight, and he'd been interpreting for the preachers almost nonstop since breakfast. Likely as not he'd get no more sleep once Oo-Pain-Shey started talking.

He pulled on his boots and the two of them crept over the rough ground, picking their way between the sleeping ministers in the field. Oo-Pain-Shey led Harry to the spirit house on the outer edge of the village.

"You wait here," he directed.

Harry watched him creep toward the small bamboo structure that looked like a dog kennel on stilts. The villagers were animists and gathered in this unholy spot to make their offerings and call on the spirits. Old Tall and Thin climbed the bamboo ladder leading to the spirit house and put his hand inside the small door, feeling around in the dark interior until he found a little cloth bag.

Coming back to Harry, he fumbled in the grubby-looking bag and drew out a rumpled piece of paper and handed it to Harry.

"What's it say?"

"It's a tract." Harry turned it over and held it close to the lantern that Old Tall and Thin carried. "It's a tract printed by Seventh-day Adventists telling people that Jesus is coming back to earth soon."

"That's right." Oo-Pain-Shey nodded his shaggy head. "That's me. That tells the people I'm coming again." He scanned the paper as if by looking hard he could make the curly Burmese characters reveal their message to him.

"Now, what does this one say?" He held out another grimy tract.

Harry read the title to him. "This one says that Saturday, the seventh day of the week, is the true Christian Sabbath, not Sunday."

"Yes, yes, Thakin. That's true. That's correct. Ah, Thakin, you are a wise man, as wise as a god, filled with the spirit of the gods, the wisest man I've ever met. Now tell me what this one says."

He handed Harry a piece of paper with a picture of a

Burmese woman bathing a baby, it was an advertisement for Colgate's soap, and on the back of the paper was a picture of a crown belonging to the king of England.

Harry explained to him what both the pictures were about, but Old Tall and Thin was not satisfied. "No, Thakin, it is pleasing your lordship to joke with me. You must tell me the truth. That is my crown, the one I'll wear when I come as king."

"Now look here—" Harry folded the pieces of paper and handed them back to the madman. "I suppose you picked these up around the city when you were in Rangoon. But I want to assure you that you are not Jesus, you are only a human being like the rest of us, and you need to have your sins forgiven and——"

Even though Oo-Pain-Shey was twice Harry's age, Harry talked to him in fatherly fashion and tried to convince him of his need of a Saviour. But he might as well have saved his breath. The poor man's warped brain could not take it in, and he kept on chuckling to himself as he rewrapped his precious tracts and advertisements. "Ah, Thakin, you are joking with me. You told me the truth about the first two pieces. Someday you will tell me the truth about the rest. It is a picture of my crown, I know. I know."

Harry shook his head despairingly. He surely hoped that the rest of the villagers they preached to were more sane than Old Tall and Thin. If not, they were wasting their time. Stifling a yawn, he said good night and in the darkness found his way back to his bedroll.

For ten days the meetings continued. All day and far into the night the people listened. There were many people, just as Old Tall and Thin had promised, and they listened attentively as the missionaries took turns preaching. Harry interpreted for everyone. He talked until he was hoarse, and still he had to keep on talking, telling the people what the white men said, and then telling the white men what the people said, interpreting questions and answers, back and forth, forth and back. It was tiring work, and only the grace of God gave Harry the strength to keep on going.

His reward came many years later. Long after he had

returned to Australia, friends in Burma wrote that thousands of people in the Pwo-Karen area had accepted Jesus as their Saviour, done away with their spirit houses, and joined the Seventh-day Adventist Church. "In fact," they wrote, "there are more believers in that area now than in the whole of the rest of Burma."

"God works in a mysterious way His wonders to perform," Harry exulted as he folded the letter and tucked it back into its envelope. "Who would have thought that so much good could come from mad Oo-Pain-Shey's sane idea."

YOU WERE DEAD, MR. SKINNER

22 THE HARRY who returned to Australia in 1928 was only a shadow of the robust young man who had left his homeland in 1915. Thirteen years of pioneering and battling against tropical diseases and malaria had taken their toll.

Five times the committee in Burma sent him home in an effort to recover his health. Harry was a valuable worker and they were just as eager to have his services as he was eager to devote his life and talents to God's work.

During one such voyage back to Australia the dread blackwater fever struck again. Harry's temperature rose to 105 degrees, 106, 107. His condition deteriorated so rapidly that the ship's doctor shook his head. "He'll never make it to Sydney."

Day and night the doctor and his helper stayed with their patient, doing what they could, knowing that the case was hopeless. Again Harry took a turn for the worse, and those watching over him saw him take his last shuddering breath.

The doctor bent over, feeling for his pulse. He pursed his lips and shook his head. Then he hooked his stethoscope into his ears and explored Harry's chest. No sign of heartbeat.

But the doctor was unaware that Harry's friends were importuning God to spare his life, and while he hesitated, about to reach for the sheet and draw it up over Harry's face and pronounce him dead, Harry's eyelids flickered.

The doctor's eyes widened. He gave a startled gasp and reached for his stethoscope again. A faint heartbeat. With renewed energy he worked over his patient.

Hours later the doctor said to Harry, "You were dead, Mr. Skinner. For about twelve minutes you were dead, and then, inexplicably, you came around again. I don't understand it."

"I do." Harry's pale lips quivered. "My work is not yet finished."

Harry was wrong. His work in his beloved Burma ended a short time later. The anopheles mosquitoes won, and Harry had to return permanently to his homeland.

But Harry was also right. His work for the Lord and for his fellow men did not end there, he simply transferred his activities from one country to another.

Harry is an *"Oo*-Thakin" now, an *old* white man. Or would it be better to say, a white man grown old in the service of his Master?

For Harry Skinner's faith and courage shine as brightly now as they did in the long ago days in India and Burma.